Excel 2019

A BASIC GUIDE FOR BEGINNERS, THE REAL BIBLE

TO LEARN FORMULAS, METHODS, AND USE OF

VBA

Page intentionally left Blank.

Table of Contents

INTRODUCTION

If you have ever managed a budget by using paper, pencil, and calculator, you would know the limitations:

1. Filling out ledger sheets

2. Calculating and recalculating totals

3. Redesigning sheets to add or delete columns and rows, and so on.

The beauty of Excel is its ability to simplify these tasks. Working with a paper spreadsheet is complicated, time-consuming, and limited. If a portion of your row data changes, you must erase and re-enter it, then you have to erase and recalculate derived data, such as totals or averages that were affected by your changes. Excel can be used to make quick and easy financial analysis, analyze data and create a presentation with chats (graph utilities), retrieve data from external data sources and use it in worksheets to calculate based on data from multiple worksheets, create a web page with ease, and run queries on data available on the web.

What is Microsoft excel?

Microsoft excel is a full-featured spreadsheet program that allows you to organize data, complete calculations, make decisions, transform data to graph, and develop professional-looking reports. The three major parts of excel are:

Worksheets

Worksheets allow you to enter, calculate, manipulate, and analyze data such as numbers and text.

Charts

Charts pictorially represent data. Excel can draw two-dimensional and three-dimensional column charts, pie charts, and other types of charts.

Databases

Databases manage data. For example, once you enter data onto a worksheet, Excel can sort the data, search for specific data, and select data that meets certain criteria.

Excel and database management

Excel is not a database package but has some special database features like sorting, filtering, and data retrieval, which allows users to create and manage the list. Hence, excel is equipped to handle and manipulate small databases. While creating a small database, two points must be noted:

The rows of data should be continuous to facilitate the manipulation of data. That is no blank row, even a column label, and the first record in the database.

The names of the columns should be entered in a single cell and must be unique.

How to start Excel

Exploring the windows

Two types of windows appear on your desktop:

The application window and the document window.

The application window contains the running program, and they have menu bars. The document window appears inside the application window, and it does not have menu bars.

The status bar

This is usually located and appears at the bottom of the screen. It shows the mode (status) of the worksheet. Take note of the word ready on the status bar that tells you that excel is ready and awaiting your next command.

All indicators that appear on the status bar at the lower right corner of the screen are:

Ready: This shows that Excel is ready for the next command.

Num: Toggles to activate the numeric keypad.

Caps: Toggles between the uppercase and the lowercase.

Scrl: Indicates that the scroll lock is on, the insertion point is not moved.

Ext: Indicates that you are in the extension mode (press f8, press ESC to deactivate).

End: Used with the navigation keys to move to the far ends, but to a1 with home key.

Edit: Press either f2 or double-click a cell to enter the edit mode.

Point: When in point mode. This is done by using either mouse or arrows to select cells instead of typing when entering formulas.

Auto-calculate: Auto-calculate is a feature located at the right side of the status bar that automatically provides averages, count, count nums, max, min, or sum for the selected data. The sum is the default formula but can be changed by right-clicking this feature on the status bar to choose any other one from the auto-calculate pop-up menu. The answer appears on the status bar.

Working in the spreadsheet

Workbooks

Workbooks are like notebooks. When excel first opens, a workbook is opened. Within that workbook are worksheets. You create your spreadsheets on the worksheets. Worksheets are organized into a rectangular grid containing columns (vertical) lettered a to iv and rows (horizontal) numbered 1 to 65,536.

A letter above each column identifies each column, with each row marked by a number on the left side of the grid. Each worksheet has 256 columns and 65,536 rows in a workbook.

Note that the alphabets in the columns can be changed to numbers by working in r1c1.

Tools - options - general tab - check r1c1 - ok.

Navigating/selecting in the worksheet.

To move to a specific cell or range, you can use the mouse, the menu, or the keyboard.

Þ to select a single cell, place your cursor on the cell, and click once (active cell).

Þ to select multiple continuous cells first make one cell the active cell. Hold the left mouse button and drag until all the desired cells are highlighted or select the first cell + shift/f8 + to select the last cell.

Þ to select an entire column/row or multiple columns/rows, select the column/row heading(s).

Þ to select entire work area/worksheet, click on the select all buttons located at the intersection between row and column headings in the upper-left corner of the worksheet

Þ to select non-contiguous areas, use ctrl with the methods of selection.

Þ you can also use the keyboard navigation keys (4 arrows, home, end, page up, page down, tab). Note that the end mode moves to the end of the data on a worksheet. e.g., ctrl+home key taken to cell a2.

Þ you can move quickly across the worksheet by using f5, ctrl + g, or edit.

È go to

Þ use the name box to specify the cell(s) and press enter e.g. single-cell a5, or range (contiguous) or range (non-contiguous)a1:b12, h13:v67, ab1:az20.

Þ use the sheet tabs to select the desired sheet(s) using other key combinations (Shift and/or ctrl).

Þ use the tab scroll buttons (located left to the sheet tabs) to navigate through the worksheets. Þ to activate any workbook of the recently opened books, window-click the desired workbook.

In a range selection, the active cell appears white and receives any keystroke. You can change the position of the active cell within a selection using enter or Shift + enter (to move down/up), tab key, or shift + tab key (to move right/left).

When you use the scroll bar, as you drag the scroll box, scroll tips appear beside the scroll bar to indicate which row will be at the top of the screen when you release the mouse button.

Cells

The point where a row and a column meet is a cell, the cell is the basic unit of the worksheet, and data is entered into cells. A cell is referred to by its unique address, or cell reference or cell indicator, which is composed of the coordinates of the intersection of a column and a row. To identify a cell, specify the column letter first, followed by the row number. For example, cell reference d3 refers to the cell located at the intersection of column d and row 3. the active cell has a heavy border surrounding the cell. Also, the active cell is listed in the reference area immediately above column a. range of cells is identified by using a1:b14, i.e., cell a1 through b14. to give a cell a unique name, select the cell, and overtype the name in the cell reference.

Inserting and deleting a worksheet

To insert a worksheet, insert - worksheet.

To delete a worksheet, make it activate è edit è delete sheet. You could also right-click on the sheet tab to insert, delete, rename, copy, move, select all sheets, and/or give them color.

Entering data

Data is entered in cells, and the most common types of data entered are texts (labels), numbers (values), and formulas. Labels are left-justified, and if the text is longer than the width of the column, they overflow characters in adjacent cells to the right as long as

These adjacent columns contain no data. Values consist of the digits zero through nine and any one of the following special characters: + - ( ), /. $ % e and e. If a cell entry contains any other character (including spaces), they are interpreted as text and treated accordingly. To enter a fraction, type the integer, then hit the space bar and type the fraction, e.g., 1.5 = 1 ‰.

To enter only the fractional part, type a zero, space, and then the fraction, e.g., 0.5 = 0 ‰. For details on formulas, see under calculation. To enter a value/label into many cells at a time, select all the cells, type the value/text, and press ctrl + enter. Values longer than 11 characters within a cell by default will be displayed as scientific notation or number sign (####). To display all the digits, widen the cell.

Note: data may be raw or derived. Raw data are entered by the user, while derived data are calculated from the raw data.

Entering numbers and texts

Any number that you enter is assumed to be a value. When you enter numbers that you don't want any calculations to be performed on them, you enter the number as a label by using the single quote before the number. For instance, both 100 and 100 will be displayed as 100 in excel but are of different formats.

Smart tags

When you make an entry that excel believes you may want to edit, a smart tag appears. This gives you the chance to make changes easily. Cells with smart tags appear with a green triangle in the upper left corner.

When you place the mouse on it, it shows an error icon that can be clicked to see the options that you can choose from concerning that data.

Editing data

After you enter data into a cell, you may want to edit it. This can be done by pressing f2, clicking in the formula bar, and double-clicking in the cell. You can change the data entry completely by just clicking the cell and enter the new data.

Anything you enter in a cell appears in both the cell and the formula bar until it is entered by accepting it. This is the entry mode. On the left part of the formula bar are three buttons: cancel, enter, and edit formulas buttons. Use the enter key, or click the enter button, or move out of the cell to accept the data entered. To reject, press escape key (ESC on the keyboard), use the cancel button, or press the backspace key to delete one character after the other. To edit, press the edit button or press f2 (this will enable you to use navigation buttons within the data).

Deleting a cell entry

Put the cursor inside the cell or highlight the group of cells and press delete.

Deleting cells, rows and columns select the rows/columns- edit- delete

Freeze titles and split panes

When a worksheet is too large to fit on the screen, you can lock some pane to remain in view while you scroll through the rest of the worksheet. Freezing titles are done to keep it in view. The titles/headings will not leave the view when scrolling through the worksheet. Select the rows or columns to be frozen. To lock window; window- freeze panes.

To unlock window; window - unfreeze panes.

Splitting the window into two or more panes.

This is done when different parts of a large worksheet are to be viewed at ones; the worksheet may be arranged vertically or horizontally, window - split. To do more, click in any of the windows where you want the split and repeat the steps.

Fill handle feature

The fill handle feature of excel makes copying formula in one cell to adjacent cells easy. The fill handle is the small rectangular box located in the lower right corner of the heavy border around the active cell. Make the active cell the cell with the formula to be copied, grab the fill handle with the mouse pointer and drag it across the cells where the formula is to be copied and applied. This can be used for filling series or copying. Using the right-click is better when the value is not continuous.

Inserting rows and columns

To insert a single row/column, select a cell in the row/column immediately below where you want to insert the new row/column- insert -rows or columns. To insert multiple rows/columns, select the same number of rows/columns that you want to insert immediately below where you want them inserted- insert- rows or columns

Adjusting row height and column width

To change the height or width of a single row/column, drag the boundary below the row/column heading until the row is the height or width you want. To change the height or width for multiple rows/columns, select the rows/columns to be change- drag a boundary below one of the selected rows until the rows are the height or width you want. Adjusting the standard column width or row height, format-rows, or columns- height or width.

Saving a file

This is similar to that of Microsoft Word. You should note that you cannot include any of the following characters in a file name: forward-slash (/), backslash (\), greater than sign (>), less than sign (<), an asterisk (*), period (.), question mark (?), quotation mark (), pipe symbol (|), colon (:), or semicolon (;).

Quitting Excel

This could be done in two ways, to exit or close from the file menu. Close to close the worksheet but exit to close the application window, i.e., file- close or exit.

Data form

When you are dealing with a worksheet with numerous columns that can't be viewed at once, to view details of a particular record, modify it or enter new data, the data form feature is used. This allows all the fields in the worksheet to be viewed at once or scroll down to view all the fields for a particular record. Data- data form

Customizing excel

Customizing settings

One of the strengths of Excel is the ability for each user to customize the program so that it works the way you want it to work. To customize excels settings, tools- options. Many of the options should not be changed from the default.

View tab

If you have a slower computer, you should consider activating the show placeholders option. This will allow you to scroll quickly through a document since objects do not have to be displayed. If you would always like to see your page breaks on your document, activate the page breaks option.

Calculation tab

If you have a large spreadsheet with a lot of formulas in it, and if you notice a delay each time you modify one of the formulas, you should consider selecting the manual option in the calculation section. With this option selected, excel will only update your calculations when you ask it to do so, instead of recalculating all formulas each time an edit is made. When you are ready to recalculate, press the f9 key.

Edit tab

One handy option allows you to dictate which cell becomes active when you press the enter key (windows). By default, when you press the enter key, the cell below the current cell becomes the active cell. You can choose to make the active cell the cell above, below, to the right or the left of the current cell. If you deselect the option, the current cell will remain the active cell when you press the enter key.

General tab

The recently used file list setting determines how many files appear at the bottom of the file menu (maximum is nine while the default is 4). The sheets in a new workbook setting determine how many blank worksheets are available in a new workbook (by default is three but can be up to 255). The standard font setting dictates the type and size of the font that will default into each new workbook. You can change the standard font type and size to your preferred font. The default file location setting tells excel where to look for files when you open an existing document. If you set this to the folder that holds all your data files, you will speed the opening of your documents.

Custom lists tab

Here you can create lists that excel uses when you copy a cell into adjacent cells using the autofill handle. For example, if you commonly create a long list of headings specific to your department, you can create a custom list to make this job easier. You can create custom lists in two ways:

1. Click a new list in the custom lists window. Then click in the list entries window and type each list member, pressing the enter key after each entry. Click the add button when you are done.

2. Create a new list by selecting a range of cells in the import list from the cells field. Once the range of cells

that contains the list is entered, click the Import button to create the new list.

Auditing

Excel offers an easy way to check your worksheets to ensure that your formulas are created correctly. With Excel, you can display tracer lines to find precedents (cells that are referred to by a formula), dependents (cells that contain formulas that refer to other cells), and errors in any cell. The first step in the process is to activate the auditing toolbar.

Tracing precedents

To determine which cells are used in the calculation of a value in another cell, select the cell with the calculated value. Click on the trace precedents button, and excel will graphically show you which cells are used in the calculation of the value in the selected cell. Click the button repeatedly, and excel will take you deeper into the precedent relationship.

Tracing dependents

To determine which cells depend on the value in a specific cell, select the specific cell. Click on the trace dependents button, and excel will graphically show you which cells rely on the value in the selected cell. Click the button repeatedly, and excel will take you deeper into the dependent relationship.

Removing precedent/dependent arrows

You can remove the arrows one level at a time by using the remove precedent arrows button and the remove dependent arrows button. You can also click the remove all arrows button to remove every arrow in the worksheet with one click.

Tracing errors

When cells return an error result, such as #value! Select the cell with that result and click the trace error button. The normal trace arrows are drawn, which enables you to track down the source of the error message.

When you see the symbol, this means that the trace extends to another worksheet or workbook. When you double click on the symbol, you will be told which workbook or worksheet has cells involved in the trace.

Validating user input

If you create worksheets that others will use to enter data, you can define rules for the data that is to be entered. If invalid data is entered, you can have automatic pop-up reminders and messages display.

Setting validation rules

To set rules, you must first access the data validation dialogue box. You do this by selecting the cells in the worksheet that are going to be subject to the rules-data- validation. The data validation dialogue box will appear. The box has three tabs.

The settings tab

In the settings tab, you set the actual rule for the selected cells. You first choose a type of data that can be entered in the allow text box, and then you complete the remaining fields on the settings tab to set the rules for that data type.

The input message tab

With this tab, you can create input messages that remind the people using the worksheet of what data is required. When a cell is selected that has an input message defined, a comment appears with the information you type in the dialogue box.

The error alert tab

Use this tab to set an error alert for those times when data entered into the cell violates the established rules.

Three types of error alerts can be defined:

Information

When displayed, the user can simply acknowledge and continue, leaving the invalid data intact.

Warning

When displayed, the user must acknowledge that they want to leave the invalid data intact

Stop

When displayed, the user must correct or reverse the entry.

Outlining

With larger worksheets, it is sometimes hard to get the big picture represented by the data. Sometimes you want to hide some of the data and only see totals. With Excel, you can create different outline levels in your worksheet. This way, you can hide or reveal the data as needed.

Creating an outline level

To create an outline level, select the rows or columns to be outlined (outlined areas cannot be immediately adjacent to other outline areas) data group and outline group. The outline is automatically created.

Using outlines

Once an outline is created, you can click on the show/hide detail buttons (the plus and minus buttons) to display or hide the contents of the outlined region.

Removing an outline level

To remove an outline level, select the rows or columns that make up the outline to be deleted-data-group and outline-ungroup. The outline is automatically deleted

Linking to m-word

You can take information from an excel worksheet and place that information into a word document. This information can be embedded in the word document or linked to the word document.

EMBEDDED VS. LINKED INFORMATION

If you embed excel information into a word document, a duplicate of the excel information is added to the Word document, thus increasing the size of the word file, and the changes in the excel document will not be reflected in the word document.

If you link excel information to a word document, a pointer is stored in the word document referencing the actual information in the excel document; this does not change the size of the word document and changes in the excel document will be displayed in the word document to reflect the current excel document.

Embedding information

Select the desired cells in excel- copy- open the word document and place the cursor at the location where you want the excel information inserted- paste.

Linking information

Select the desired cells in excel- copy- open the word document and place the cursor at the location where you want the excel information linked- paste special- paste link- select the formatted text (rtf) option- ok

Concatenation

You can join the values in two or more cells into a single cell. For instance, if you have a person's first name in one cell and their last name in a second cell, you can concatenate the cells, which will result in the full name being displayed in a single cell. Join multiple cell values into a single cell, click in the cell where we need the dataè type = first cell & & second cellèenter. You can do this for more than two cells.

Text to column

You can take a text in a single cell and break it out into multiple cells. For instance, if you have a person's name in a single cell (first name, last name) and you want to sort by the last name, you can break up the name into separate cells, and then you can sort by the last name.

To split single values into multiple cells: you must have enough empty cells to the right of the original cell to hold the data once it has been split. Select the cell with the multiple values- data- text to columns- the data will either be delimited (characters such as commas or tabs separate each value) or fixed-width (fields are aligned in columns with spaces between each field)-select the appropriate option- next- if delimited, check the box that contains the appropriate delimiter. If fixed width, insert, delete or move the vertical line so that the window shows the breaks as you desire them- next- finish single and multiple levels of sorting data,

This is done to rearrange and reorder data in a list. This is done to rearrange the records in a specified order, e.g., alphabetically, numerically, chronologically, and either ascending or descending order. The particular field must be set as a reference; this field is called sort key.

A list is an arranged collection of related information. Lists are usually arranged in a column and -row format as a labeled series of rows that contain similar data, e.g., telephone books, checkbooks, and personal phone directories.

In excel, a list must contain at least one column, which represents one category of information. Every column is recognized by a title called a column label. Common labels should contain a font, data type, alignment, formatting, pattern, border, or capitalization style that differs from the data contained in the rows beneath them. This is how the column labels are recognized.

A row in a list's called a data set. Each data set contains information from one or more columns linked to it.

Sorting is used for the alphabetical, numerical, or chronological organization of data sets in your list. When sorting a list, the rows will be ordered according to one or more column contents. If you want to rearrange the data sets in your list according to the information contained in just one column, a simple sorting can be done using the sort.

Excel selects the entire list automatically for sorting, but for formatting differences, companies select the rows in the list. If it seems that the top row is formatted differently from the next rows, it will identify that row as a column label and exclude it from the sort. You can use the command edit- undo sort to undo a sort immediately after it is executed. If you have given another order, you no longer have the undo button. If your list is not in a specific order, and you want to assign an order to it, then you can number the order sets in your list. By this, without relying on the undo button, you can quickly return to the original order.

In lists, many sets of data might contain some similar information, e.g., two or more students might have the same surname. Due to the connections that occur with repeated details, sorting the list by the data contained in one column may not provide enough order. The sort command lets you sort by multiple information columns to sever these links, the data. Consecutive sorts enable you to sort your list by more than three columns you can specify in the sort dialogue box. in consecutive sorts; you must perform the sorts for the least important order first, then work your way up to the most important sort order. The sort dialogue box enables you to specify three columns by which to sort a list. The sort-by drop-down list specifies the secondary sort order, and the second then-by drop-down list specifies the list sort order.

Custom sort

Rearrange your data in chronological order. To customize sort order, use the sort options button in the sort order dialogue box.

Automatic subtotals help to sum up the data in a table. Using an Excel summary feature like number, count, or average, you construct subtotals. To use subtotals, the data must be arranged into a correctly structured list and sorted by the column by which you wish to summarize the data.

Filtration

If you are working with a list of items as you would if you had a database in excel, you can use the auto filter tool to search through your list for particular records quickly. When filtering a list, you can only show data sets that satisfy a set of search conditions (called criteria). The auto filter feature helps you to filter out all records that meet your requirements. The list itself is unchanged, and you can change the criteria to display another set of records at any time.

Auto filtering

Select the column(s), or cell(s) è data è filter è auto filter arrows are shown on the columns from which you want to filter. Navigate through the list by using the drop-down arrow buttons to indicate individual criterion per column meeting your criteria. After you name a filter criterion for one column, you can filter your list further by selecting filter criteria for other columns. This procedure creates an and condition, i.e., the sets of data must meet all the set criteria. Although sets of data that don't meet your criteria remain in the worksheet, the rows that contain them are hidden. To display a filtered list of records-click on the desired button and select your desired criteria.

You can also select one of the following special filtering options:

All – un-filters your list and shows all records.

Top 10 (used for numbers and dates only) displays the top or bottom 10 (or another number you select) of records in the list, or the top or bottom 10% (or another number you select) of the records in the list.

Blanks

This selection allows you to display only the records with missing entries.

Nonblanks

This selection allows you to display only records that have some type of entry in the cell.

This option allows you to display criteria meeting your customized needs. State your comparison criteria by selecting the desired operator then enter the comparison value in the window on the right. You can use multiple comparison criteria by selecting the and or options and entering the desired criteria in the lower two windows. The or condition allows you to use a set of data that must meet either the first filter criteria or the second filter criteria. Use the drop-down list to select custom. This can also be used to find values that fall within a specified range by using a comparison operator.

You may use wildcards to check for data sets in a list that have some common text inside single entries, even in the entire file. Wildcard Sources include:

Asterisk (*): locates any characters in the same position as the asterisk.

Question mark?): (finds every particular character in the same position as the question mark.

Tilde (~): finds a question mark or asterisk.

Note that if some columns are selected before the auto filtering command, the drop-down arrows are only shown in the selected columns, but the filtering is applied to the entire worksheet. To display all the hidden rows so that the entire list is visible, use data è filter è show all. This removes the filtering from the worksheet. If you want to remove filtering for certain column(s), select all from the drop-down list options.

Advanced filtering

When using excel as a database, you can query information by the use of filters. Filters allow you to extract data based on the criteria you specify.

Type the headings in new space to specify below it the criteria. Values on the same line mean and condition while on different line signifies or condition.

To filter in place, you must first establish the criteria area and then input your criteria. Select the labels for all of the fields è copy these labels- select an area of the worksheet, and paste- enter the criteria you want to use to filter your database (criteria entered on the same row will be treated as an and condition. Criteria entered on different rows will be treated as an or condition.

Filter in place

To perform a filtering action that will place the search results in the location of the existing database: select any cell in your database- data- filter- advanced filter- click the collapse dialogue button to select the cells that contain the criteria (all field labels must be included) -click the collapse dialogue button to restore the dialogue box to the screen- ensure that filter the list, the in-place option is selected- ok. Filter to another location select any cell in your database-data-filter- advanced filter- click the collapse dialogue button to select the cells that contain the criteria (all field labels must be included) - click the collapse dialogue button- click the collapse dialogue button to the right of the copy to box- select in the worksheet area where you need the results-click the collapse dialogue button- ensure that copy to another location option is selected- ok.

Protection

It is fairly easy to replace a formula with a value inadvertently. To avoid having this happen to your painstakingly-crafted formulas, you can choose to lock cells and/or protect the workbook. By default, all cells are locked. Until you enable protection, however, the lock has no effect. What you must do before you protect a worksheet is to unlock all the cells for data entry or editing are to be enabled.

There are several levels of protection that you can place on a workbook. You can:

- ✓ Assign a password that is required before a file can be opened.
- ✓ Assign a password that is required to modify a file.
- ✓ Set up the file so that it is recommended as a read-only file. \
- ✓ Hide worksheets in a workbook and require a password to be used to re-display the worksheets.
- ✓ Protect specific cells within a workbook so that changes cannot be made to the cells.

Microsoft's history boasts.

The most efficient, customizable, and widely used solution for business.

MSExcel has been around since 1982, first introduced as multi-plan, a very popular cp / m (microcomputer control program) but lost popularity to lotus 1-2-3 on ms-dos systems. Microsoft introduced Excel v2.0 for windows in 1987 and started outselling lotus 1-2-3 and emerging quatropro in 1988. In 1993, Microsoft released Excel v5.0 for windows that included VBA, aka macros. This opened up almost unlimited possibilities for the automation of repetitive tasks for numbers crunching, process automation, and business data presentation.

MICROSOFT EXCELS TODAY

Microsoft Excel is the most familiar, flexible, and widely used business application in the world thanks to its ability to adapt to almost any business process. There is nothing that can't be done by this very strong combination, combined with the use of other Microsoft Office software, word, outlook, PowerPoint, etc.

Microsoft uses excel, and the office suite is nearly limitless. Let's consider the top 10 list of the most popular and powerful features built-in Excel:

1. Effectively model and evaluate practically any data

1. Quickly zero in on the right data points

3. Build single-cell data charts

4. Connect your spreadsheets from almost anywhere

5. Link, share and achieve more when working together

6. Profit from more collaborative and intuitive swivel charts

7. Bring more depth to the presentations of the data

8. Do things quicker and easier

9. Harness more power to create bigger, more complex tablets

10. Publish and exchange Services Excel

Add to that now the ability to configure and automate any process using VBA, and you have a huge value-added bi (business intelligence) platform that is versatile and innovative enough to deal with business needs and needs.

The prospect of Excellence

Where are we going from here? With the internet being more important to our lives and business, it makes sense to dominate over the needs of the many. With the recent introduction of PowerPivot, which is used to access much larger data sets, the row/column cap is extended from 64k to 1 m, and the path is clear for Microsoft office web apps. Excel's integration with the ctp Hadoop connector for SQL server is currently being developed and tested, enabling the seamless integration of older and newer technology with much more extensive data set usage capabilities for bi.

Business is moving ever more towards cloud-based computing for data and collaboration accessibility shears. This is where we see Microsoft's future excellence shifting to breakneck speed in the next few years to provide multi-user access to massive data for analysis, reporting, and substantial efficiency and production increases.

Custom solutions are needed in today's dynamic business climate to maintain the edge over competition and profits. Microsoft Excel consultancies are the leaders of today's and emerging technologies. Finding a professional retainer consultant is of vital importance in harnessing the maximum power and efficiencies required to succeed in the 21st century.

WHAT'S NEW ABOUT EXCEL 2019?

Microsoft revealed earlier this autumn the launching of its Office 2019 suite to the general public. Excel's 2019 edition contains a large variety of new and improved functionality and capabilities. Here's a look at 12 of those updates, all downloaded, activated, and checked by me:

1. **Improvements to the data import tool**: The Power Query data import tool in Excel 2013 was renamed Get & Transform in Excel 2016, but the name returned to Power Query in Excel 2019 following the naming conventions used for the associated Microsoft Power Pivot, Power Map and Power BI products. The improved Power Query tool (pictured below) offers the ability to import data from external data. The ability to put data in groups, rename column headings, transpose data, reverse rows, identify data types, delete values, break columns, merge columns, unpivot columns, invoke

custom functions, construct conditional columns and parse data are some of the transforming capabilities.

This method makes the import of data from external sources for manipulation and analysis in Excel quicker, simpler, and more precise.

2. **Automated workflow**: Excel 2019 now integrates better with Microsoft Flow, which allows you to construct automated workflows in which data is extracted from other applications and then stored and/or manipulated in Excel. Furthermore, the data flow can be designed to automatically submit or share the data with other people or third party applications. For example, Flow may be used to collect favorable customer tweets on your Twitter account about your products or services, and then store them in your Excel workbook (on your OneDrive or SharePoint platform). These Twitter data could then be sent to selected recipients regularly (e.g., every Monday morning) via email or text messages, or released directly to websites or other destinations for data.

Flow can get the data from almost anywhere — the accounting system, ERP system, CRM system, stock price databases, weather forecast databases, email messages, recall notifications, Salesforce.com, etc. You may use this technology as examples to monitor your working hours, travel locations, Facebook messages, Instagram updates, travel expenses, receivable accounts, etc. Start the My Flows web page at login.microsoftonline.com to create a new data flow, sign in to your account using your Microsoft ID, and click the Start button.

Click Create a blank flow as pictured below in the bottom right corner, then pick one of more than 200 triggers and choose the event you want your automated flow method to begin. For example, an email receipt with a particular attachment may activate an automated flow process. Continue by defining the action(s) you want to take, such as opening the email attachment in Excel and running a different macro to generate a PivotTable or PivotChart, then specify a connection to share the results via other Microsoft and third-party applications such as Outlook or SharePoint. Get more information on Flow at click.linksynergy.com.

3. **3D images**: Excel 2019 also offers a new 3D image feature, where you can rotate an object's 3D model. Although it is difficult to express the idea in a frame, there are three copies of the same butterfly image in the screenshot below, which I have rotated to show the effect you might achieve.

Excel now contains hundreds of 3D images, accessible from the 3D Models option on the Insert page. Categories of images include animals, electronics, gadgets, dinosaurs, geology, space, dioramas, letters, biography, and more. The screenshot below provides a few examples of 3D graphic images.

4. **Custom functions:** With Excel 2019, users can now build their own custom functions using JavaScript. Previous editions of Excel have allowed users to create user-defined functions using the built-in programming language of Excel's Visual Basic for Applications; however, since JavaScript has emerged as a widely used platform for such purposes, Microsoft has added this new capability to enable greater compatibility with third-party solutions.

5. **New functions**: Excel contains the following six new or modified functions: IFS, Move, 5-0TEXTJOIN, CONCAT, MAXIFS, and MINIFS. The IFS and Turn versions of the nested IF feature are simpler, removing the need for more complex nested functions. For example, the screenshot below shows both the nested IF approach (in red text) and the IFS approach (in blue text) to create the formula in cell C16 that returns the proper income tax base. The IFS approach needs only one function, while the IF approach requires three IF functions, while both approaches operate. Note that the IFS approach in this example generates a slightly longer formula since the IFS approach requires that you define each criterion, while the IF approach does not require that you define the last criterion.

The TEXTJOIN feature is a simplified version of the CONCATENATE function where quotation marks need not encapsulate the inserted text. The CONCAT function allows you to combine text from multiple cells without having to define a delimiter. The MAXIFS and MINIFS functions work like the

SUMIF or COUNTIF functions in that for those data that meet the requirements, you define they measure only the limit or minimum. For example, as part of statistical sampling procedures, an auditor may use these functions to find the lowest and highest invoice amounts between $50 and $100.

6. **Customized visuals**: Microsoft has incorporated its Power BI suite of apps into Excel to provide more visual ways to display and present your data. To access these new design visuals, select Get Add-ins from Excel's tab to view the Office Add-ins dialogue box.

Scroll through the applications, pick the one you want to use, then configure the device to connect it to the data you want. I selected the free Microsoft People Graph software, for example, to build the chart below as linked from the data shown in cells A1: B5.

Other visual add-in apps available include Word Cloud charts, Bullet charts, Speedometer charts, Prevedere Forecasting Tools, Excel Lucidchart Diagrams, and, to name a few, Supermetrics.

Note: As of September 2018, I have counted more than 350 available Excel add-in applications; more apps could be added. (Most of these add-in applications are free, although others are priced from $1.49 to $13.99, and some are priced from $1.49 to $5.99 a month.)

7. **Complete SVG graphics support**: Excel 2019 now supports scalable vector graphics (SVG), meaning your graphic images do not pixelate as you increase the image size, as demonstrated in the screenshot below with the small and larger hiker picture. (Note that this technology only applies to graphic images and drawings; it does not apply to pictures, videos, or animations.)

8. **500 + new built-in icons**: Excel provides 500 + new built-in SVG-compliant dashboards and infographics icons; examples of the latest walker and mountain icons are shown above.

9. **New forms capabilities**: Excel 2019 now works in conjunction with Microsoft Forms to generate better-looking documents to ask for answers to questions like those used in surveys, polls, and quizzes. Using

this new technology, for example, you can create survey forms, and distribute them through Excel links. To start creating a new form, visit forms.office.com, sign in if necessary, and click on the New Form button (if this is your first visit, you may see an overlay screen with a −Create a new form button).

As you gather automatic responses, the survey results in Excel can be opened for further review or charting of the data collected.

10. **Improvements to the map chart**: New options allow you to project your maps in layouts of Albers, Mercator, or Miller (which means you can display your map chart as flat or curved). There are also new controls to pick the region of the map to view. You can show a world map, for example, even though the data span only the USA.

11. **Chart enhancements:** In Excel 2019, new options allow you to monitor better the axis information on your funnel charts, such as tick marks and number formats, and you can now also generate color-coded heat maps.

12. **Co-authoring**: New co-authoring features allow you to share your workbooks with others, enabling several users to edit the same workbook at the same time as your file is stored on either the SharePoint or OneDrive platform. The collaboration tool also lets you set collaborator permissions, and workbooks can be shared with individuals or user groups (see the screenshot below).

WHY LEARN TO USE EXCEL 2019?

Analysts, consultants, advertisers, banks, and accountants all make regular use of excel. You may also notice that other random people, such as graphic designers and engineers, are working on the strong formulas and charts with excellent.

Seeing how outstanding the workplace is so famous, it's worth learning all about it and getting the experience on your CV. You can find your current degree doesn't produce any job opportunities, so moving into Excel could meanwhile get you a job.

Excellent Fundamentals

Microsoft Excel 3.0 Ad 1991-92, Microsoft Sweden

It's important to learn the fundamentals of excel if you want a solid base for advanced functionality. Here are a few tools to get you going, even though you've never used excel before:

Excellent quick website: this tutorial gets you going with Microsoft Excellent, without jargon and technical words overboard. It begins with things like assembling cells, finding ribbons and workbooks, and using keyboard shortcuts to speed the editing process.

Youtube Motion Training Channel: offers a convincing place to start your work, as the beginner video is only nine minutes long, and you have visuals to follow along. The course for beginners has four parts, so you can split it into pieces and make notes while you move around if you need to reference it back.

Get started Microsoft's guide: delivers a three-part video course with data entry and spreadsheet editing necessary. It also includes color-coding and data bars, along with information on how to create charts and pivot tables.

Then work with cells, sheets, data, formulas, and functions move on. Provides information about how to buy Microsoft Excel, as well as a list of new features in recent updates.

Chandoo: get intermediate information on conditional formatting and quickly produce reports.

Within this one bok, the bare basics are illustrated, using some text, photos, and video. Yet, it also has some additional tools for you to browse through and read more.

This excellent made beginner's guide easy: accessible from keynote support, this tutorial dives into questions like "What is Microsoft Excel?" While it may sound incredibly simplistic, it's a good question to ask while you're trying to know. There's also a wonderful version of a basic excel worksheet structure. That way, when knowing the excellent words and shortcuts, you know exactly where to go.

Excellent exposure: Online training course with links to many video lessons is free. Conditional formatting and testing for errors are just some of the topics covered in the earlier sections and go all the way to macros and some more advanced details. Excel Visibility has a wide audience. You will communicate with certain people and ask questions in the comments that really get answers.

Excellent guru99 tutorials: offers answers to questions about excellence features, visualizes data maps, excels in the cloud, discrepancies between csv and exc. It has some topics that you can't find anywhere else, and with beautiful images and animations, it's all online.

Excel wiki how to use wow: this could be one of your first moves if you're a complete novice with Microsoft excel. Also, if it's not all that detailed, the guide focuses on the real basics with screenshots zooming in areas and arrows to guide you. This includes everything from the printing of the Excel sheet to the completion of simple functions in an easy-to-read format.

Basic Excel software page: Only experienced users need a refresher in Excel's simpler software, and it's a good tool for handy usage. You may need to find out, for example, what the find and replace feature is. A fast search through this article will get you to the answer.

Advanced Algebra tutorials

It helps to learn advanced mathematics when dealing with numbers and formulas so that you learn what's possible in excel. Such tools include a refresher for real-world use cases of mathematics:

Excellent advanced formulas and functions: this course has been viewed thousands of times, and it takes only six hours to complete, including photos, downloadable materials, and a transcription. Exercise files enhance the way you study, as you are given the opportunity to practice during the course.

Excellent math functions: this list is a good starting point for those interested in learning functions except the most basic. It goes further into the more advanced users, and when you make your own formulas in excel, you get a whole selection of what to expect.

Texas University of Applied Sciences website: contains advanced formulas and functions, including financial formulae and conditional functions. Some other functions that might be important to you include len, correct, trim, and rounding. The segment on financial formulas is especially interesting for those wishing to work in the accounting or banking field.

Top Twenty-five Microsoft Excel advanced formulas: hands-on tutorial: if you want to have the majority of the knowledge you need in one place, it might be wise to pay for the udemy course. Each one has trained more than 9,000 students, including courses to learn the top 25 most complex mathematical formulas in excel. It gives examples of the formulas in the real world, and you can see how to use them in the future.

Microsoft Excel – advanced formulas & functions: another amazing class of udemy with tricks and tips for the real world. The course claims it's best for analysts, covering more than 75 of the most complex formulae in excel. Dozens of pdf quizzes, hands-on files, and slides are available for download, and there's a beautifully designed course outline to guide you through some of the more challenging techniques.

Excel as a financial calculator: this book is especially useful since not everyone has a real financial calculator to work with. In reality, most of the time, you 're on your Microsoft Excel Open machine. And knowing these functions in several fields makes sense. We like the key, which compares some of the more advanced features to buttons on a financial calculator in excel. This helps you to move smoothly from a calculator to an Excel spreadsheet.

Great exposure: offers a comprehensive, outstanding tutorial starting with a table introduction and a wide variety of math and statistical functions. You will learn roundup, countif, round down, countblank, median, and much more, for starters. Excel presentation keeps the posts on the shorter side, which is nice if you want the material to be consumed in small help.

Advanced time and math calculations: practical guides supplied primarily in video format. All the calculations are done by excel, and you can see the graphics and practice them at your own time. The videos are also short, so when you get going, you're not intimidated.

Tutorial Server

Excel is not just about spreadsheets. They can also be used for databases. Getting familiar with the databases will help you work out how to use some of the more complicated features of excel:

Microsoft office tutorial about importing data into Excel and building a data model: one of the key reasons people use Excel is for data mining and general building databases. This builds on the fundamentals of data inclusion and subsequently organizes such data. The tutorial is broken down into many easy-to-understand links, so it's not that hard to skip around. You might, for example, start by learning how to import data using copy and paste, then go straight to create a relationship with the imported data.

Construction of a database in excel with a table or a list: wonder how to provide a few easy video tutorials for those interested in this subject. It's just about the most simple you can get with Excel databases, and the videos are brief enough to not confuse you with the content from the beginning.

Using excel as your database: A good chandoo tutorial. Includes gifs animated to complement the text. This speeds up the learning process, because the photos are zoomed in for a more interactive guide, but still moving. It also describes the application module, which is an important concept of the entire process of databasing. Be warned that some of the photos come from older versions of Excel.

Setting up the Excel database: the primary course is just around an hour, and it is run by Excel Expert Dennis Taylor. Several issues include the use of formulas, sliders to allow table filtering and the use of data validation to limit data entry. These topics come with certain accessible types of knowledge and practice.

Best Excel tutorial: Explore database functions with the most popular feature you 'd ever use to construct or min a database. Some headers contain such functions as dmin, dproduct, dvarp, and dvar, for example.

How to build a database in excel: begin with an overview of the database and move on to other more advanced topics such as filtering data and completing database format. The formatting portion is one of the most critical sections, as the whole database point is intended for real-world use. If creating a database doesn't translate into the real world, you've never mastered that.

Functions Microsoft Outstanding

You have to be able to write the functions to understand how to use Excel fully. Upon learning the basics, you'll be able to build powerful spreadsheets that unlock the tool's true strength.

The 10 most widely used functions in Excel: a good place to get the ball rolling, so you don't have to tackle any issues or worksheets. All shown in the video is a tutorial.

GCF Learn Free: Another nice guide with all the formulas that you should know. This is a fantastic tool for bookmarking, as the majority of real-world functions are illustrated here. You get free access to the guides, and the videos and articles are all set up.

Some of these topics include "practice reading formulas," "percentage off sales," and "use if feature."

Excellent formulas and functions: Excellent simple tutorial, beginning with copying and pasting and going all the way to adding a function. These are the real essentials, but to others, it can seem a little simplistic.

Comprehensive list of just about every feature you might think of: this is technically not a guide, but it's going to be helpful as you work through some of the others on the list. It begins with count and number, where you can click on the link to show the relevant formulas. The website has many other figures, financial categories, and more.

15 Excel shortcuts widely used: this is a PCWorld cheat sheet that contains formulas, too. It serves as a simple reference point for anyone needing it.

Excellent instructions to graphing

You can automatically build graphs and charts with your data after you have your figures and formulas in excel:

Ncsu: addresses most graphical specifications with links to the bar graphs and histograms topics. This includes the import of text files, along with the most basic of graphs for those just starting.

Ways to create a chart or graph in Excel

The Tutorial offers a series of free excel models. This increases the graphics used as it shows graphs in their full form and asks you to return them.

Build a map with Excel Easy: instructions to help you make a graph of the wildlife population and see how it can be done by a student or someone in the wildlife business.

MS office tutorial: This is one of the best tutorials, as it teaches you how to create a chart from beginning to end. Part of the tutorial is achieved through a video, but much of the learning comes from a large article with pictures and suggestions of shifting the map, resizing, and showing a legend.

Build advanced charts: guru99 is renowned for advanced tutorials, and this one is no different. The guide addresses the importance of advanced maps but also focuses on topics such as creating combinations and adjusting axis headings.

Excellent tutorials for perception

It can be difficult to print data from Excel, particularly if you have a very large sheet. Those services will help you get the smooth, organized print you need:

Print a worksheet: this super simple article delves into the most common method of printing in the world of excellence.

Workbook printing: this subject may sound overwhelming, but chandoo has covered you with a five-minute video and some other related items such as converting excel to pdf and printing excellent cell comments.

How to print with gridlines in Excel: answers a query many people have on their excellent journey. For several fields, the grid lines are useful, but this device seems to be buried in excel. The good news is that getting the job done takes just about a minute.

Excellent Tutorial programming

Use these programming tools to learn advanced functions in excel.

Home and learn: provides a full, free course loaded with tutorials on how to master VBA programming through excel. Strings, loops, and lists, along with variables and conditional logic, are all protected here.

Corporate Excellent Tutorials

Specifically designed to fine-tune your knowledge of Excel for business use:

Excellent with business: Your go-to stop with the help of excel to develop your career. The course on business analysis talks about transforming data buckets into sound business decisions and taking those data and making them important to other business people.

Advanced Excel Programme: useful for those who have been educated in the past but want to go to more of a "graduate school" for business excellence.

Synopsis

Excel is one of Microsoft's most popular office suite devices, so understanding how it works will boost your job opportunities, so allow you to be more comfortable in using mathematics. As you know, those tools will help you.

SOFTWARE GLOSSARY & HOW TO USE EXCEL 2019 (BASIC)

Not sure what the difference between a workbook and a workbook is? How do you know whether or not a cell is active? You really aren't safe. Understanding the words used in excel requires knowledge in excel the possibilities.

Microsoft Excel Terms

Workbook — The workbook refers to the spreadsheet program Excel. The workbook includes all the data you entered and enables you to arrange or quantify the results. A workbook that is available for viewing and editing by multiple network users is known as a shared workbook.

Worksheet — You'll find papers called worksheets inside the workbook. Often known as spreadsheets, several worksheets can be nestled in your workbook. At the bottom of the page, tabs will display which of your worksheets you're working on. That is often referred to as an active worksheet or panel.

Cell — a cell is a triangle or a rectangle enclosed in a worksheet. Any data you wish to enter in your worksheet shall be stored in a cell. Cells can be color-coded; they can show text, numbers, and calculation results depending on what you want to do. An active cell is currently available to edit.

Columns and rows- columns and rows refer to the orientation of the cells. Columns are aligned vertically, while rows are horizontally aligned.

Column and row headings — these headings are grey areas of letters and numbers located just outside the columns and rows. Pick the complete row or column by clicking on a heading. The headings may also be used to adjust the row height or column width.

Workspace — similar to worksheets in a workbook, a workspace helps you to access can file at once.

Ribbon — a portion of command tabs called ribbon is above the workbook. There are several options behind each tab of the ribbon.

Cell reference — a cell reference is a set of coordinates representing a specific cell. This is a combination of letters and numbers. For example, a5 will indicate the cell where column a and row 5 intersect.

Cell range — the cell range consists of a set of cells classified as a category based on a number of criteria. Excel will evaluate the number, also known as an array, by using a colon (:) between the cell references. For example, a range in a row might look like a1: c1, telling the formula to look at cells in a row between a1 and c1, while b4: d9 will tell the formula to look at all cells in columns b and d and rows 4 and 9. A 3-d relation refers to a range in the same workbook, which includes more than one worksheet.

Merged cell — when two or more cells are fused, what is known as a merged cell is such.

Model — a model is a structured workbook or worksheet designed to help users fulfill a particular requirement of excel. Examples include product analysis, process map, and calendar.

Operator — Operators are symbols or signs showing which calculation the expression should be used for. Operators do not generally refer to simple mathematical types; there is also a compare, text concatenation, or comparison operator.

Formula — a sequence used to generate value within a cell. It must start with a sign equal to (=). It can be a mathematical equation, a reference cell, a function, or an operator. An expression is also known as the formula.

Formula bar — nestled between the ribbon and the workbook, the formula bar shows the activated cell contents. For formulas, the Formula bar shows all formula components.

Task — the functions are formulas which are pre-constructed to excel. They are designed to help clarify formulas which are potentially complicated in the worksheet.

Error code — error codes will appear when excel can find an issue with the formula given.

Cell formatting — this is the Shift in the cell data displayed in the table. Only the external appearance of cells is changed when you format cells; the meaning inside the cells remains unchanged.

Conditional formatting — formatting shall only be enforced if the cell meets other conditions, such as duplicate values or values above or below a threshold.

Filter — Filters are rules which you can use to decide which rows to view in a worksheet. Those filters can use data such as terms or values.

Freeze panes — Freeze panes allow you to pick different columns and/or rows to remain visible on the worksheet, even while scrolling, such as column header cells.

Autofill — this helps you to copy data to more than one cell without effort.

Autosum — this feature adds the numbers you entered into your sheet and shows the total number in the cell of your choosing.

Autoformat — it's an automatic application format for cells that follow pre-determined requirements. That may be as basic as the orientation and size of the font.

Data validation — this feature helps avoid the insertion of incorrect data into your worksheet. This is most widely used for creating drop-down lists of specific words. Validation of data shall foster the quality and accuracy of the data to be entered.

Pivot table — this is the most widely used data review method for sorting and the average for automatically summing up results. The data is taken from one table, while the results are shown in another row. Pivot tables simplify the extraction of relevant information from a broad database.

Pivot map — Visual assistance for pivot tables is given by this form of graphic. The consumer can have a degree of interactivity with the data by providing a graphical representation of the pivot table data.

Pivot area — the pivot area is the point on the worksheet where you can drag a pivot table field to rearrange the view of a chart.

Source data — this is the knowledge the pivot table is built with. It may exist either within a worksheet or from an external database.

Area values — value areas are defined in a pivot table as the cells containing the summary information.

Item — these are the sub-field groups in your pivot table. If you have a field labeled with the state, the things will be Alabama, Alaska, etc.

To tie-up

While there are so many other things to cover for Microsoft Excel, the list above will get you on the right track to become a titan table. If you first started using excel, what words did you trip over? Are there any more words for this list that you would suggest? Let's let us know!

Where to hire Excel 2019

Excel is a strong app — but it can be very intimidating too.

That's why we put together this guide for beginners to get started with Excel.

It takes you from the very beginning (opening a spreadsheet), through data entry and function, and finishes with data saving and sharing.

It's everything you need to learn to continue excelling.

This guide is for windows to excel in 2019. Did they have a different version? No issue, you still have the exact same steps to take.

Opening a worksheet

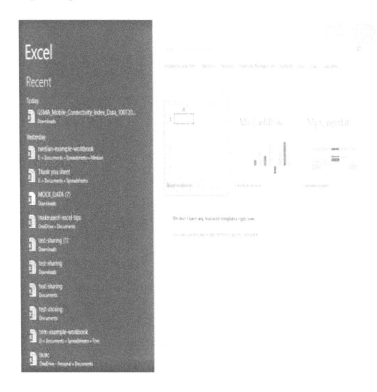

Whenever you open Excel for the first time (by double-clicking the icon or choosing it from the start menu), the program will ask what to do.

Click on the blank workbook if you wish to open a new spreadsheet.

Click on Open Other Workbooks in the lower-left corner to open an existing spreadsheet (like the sample workbook you just downloaded), then press Browse on the left side of the resulting window.

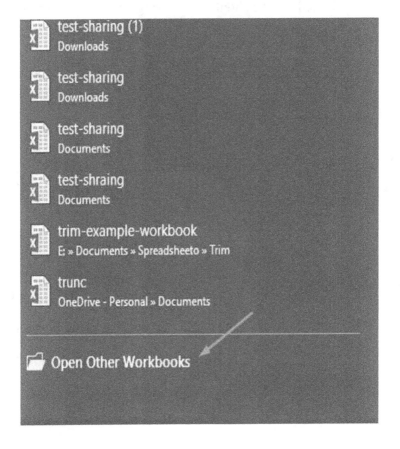

Then use the Explorer file to find the workbook you are searching for, pick it and press Open.

Workbooks vs. Tablets

Something we should be clearing up before we move forward.

An Excel file is a Workbook. Typically it has a.xlsx file extension (if you're using Excel's older version, it may be.xls).

Single sheet spreadsheet inside a workbook. Most sheets may be inside a workbook and accessed via the tabs at the bottom of the page.

Playing with the Band

The Excel main control panel is a cord. You can do just about everything directly from the ribbon you like.

Where's the mighty tool? Upside the window:

A spreadsheet showing:

	A	B	C	D	E	F
1	45	37				
2	21	4				
3	-34	17				
4	1	0				
5	Welcome to	Spreadsheeto				
6						
7						
8						

There are a variety of tabs like home, insert, analysis, info, and a few more. Every tab has its own buttons.

Start clicking on a few tabs to see which buttons appear underneath.

There is a very handy ribbon search bar, too. It says tell me what you'd like to do. Only type in what you're searching for an Excel you'll find.

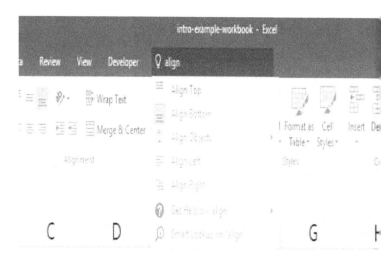

You will most of the time be in the ribbon's Home tab. But formulae and data are also very useful (we're going to think about formulae soon).

Pro tip: Ribbon unit

The ribbon also has several smaller pieces, in addition to the tabs. And those parts will help you find something unique when you're searching for it.

If you are searching for sorting and filtering solutions, for example, you don't want to swing over hundreds of buttons to find out what they're doing.

Instead, scroll through the names of the segment before you find what you want:

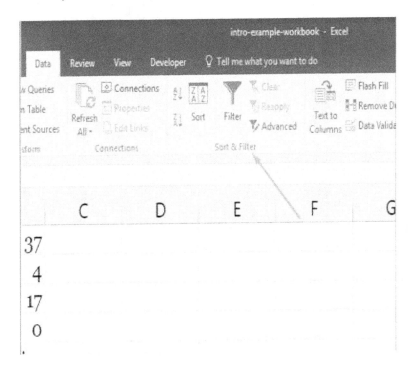

Manage the files

Workbooks, as we have shown, will contain several sheets.

Those sheets can be handled with sheet tabs near the bottom of the panel. Click on a tab to open a similar worksheet.

If you use our workbook example, you will see two papers, which are called welcome and thank you

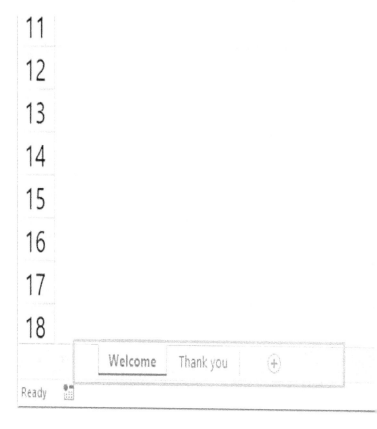

Click the + button at the extreme of the sheet list to add a new worksheet.

The sheets in your workbook may also be reordered by moving them to a new location.

And if you right-click on the tab of the worksheet, you will be given a range of options:

Don't think about those choices too much for now. Rename and delete is helpful, so you don't need to be concerned about the rest.

Putting in data

Now is the time to fill in some details!

And while data entry is one of the most critical and core things to do in excel, it's almost effortless.

Only press the blank cell and get started typing.

Go ahead and try! Type in some blank cells, your name, birthday, and favorite.

You can also

Copy using (ctrl c),

cut (ctrl x), and

paste (ctrl v) any data you want to try copying and pasting data from the spreadsheet example into a specific section.

You can also copy data from other excel programs.

Try copying and pasting this list of numbers into your folder:

17

24

9

00

3

12

That's what we'll cover for baseline data entry. Only know there's a lot of other ways to bring data into your spreadsheets when you need it.

Edge calculations

Now that we have seen how to get some simple data into our computer, we'll do some stuff with that.

It is easy to run simple calculations on excel. Next, we'd be looking at how to connect two digits.

Important: Calculations start with = (equals)

Once you run a calculation (or a formula that we're going to explore next), the first thing you need to type is the equals symbol. This tells Excel to get some sort of calculation ready to run.

And when you see something like = median (a2: a51), make sure you type it as it is — including the equals symbol.

Let's bring in 3 and 4. Into a blank cell type the following formula:

$= 4 + 3$

Then reach for **ENTER**.

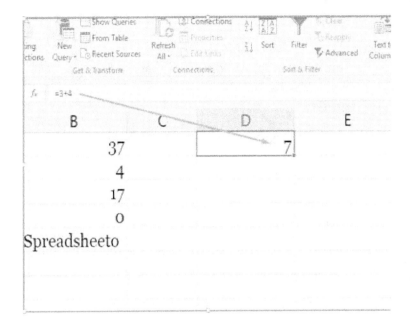

Excel tests the equation when you click enter, and shows the answer: 7.

Yet if you look at the formula bar above, the original formula is yet to be seen.

This is a good thing to recall if you forget what you originally wrote.

You may also edit the formula bar to a cell. Click each of the cells, then click on the formula bar to start typing.

It is just as simple to perform the subtraction, multiplication, and division. Test the formulae here:

= 4–6

= 2 * 5 Figures

= -10/3 —-

Where we're going to cover next in Excel is one of the most important items. We 're giving you a very simple summary here, but do not hesitate to read our cell references post to get the information.

Let's just try something new now. Open the first sheet of a workbook illustration, click on cell c1, and type the following:

= A1+b1

CLICK ON ENTER.

In cells a1 and b1, you will get 82, the sum of the numbers.

Now, change one number to a1 or b1 and look at what happens:

	A	B	C	D
A1			f_x 45	
1	45	37	82	
2	21	4		
3	-34	17		
4	1	0		
5	Welcome to	Spreadsheeto		
6				
7				

Since you are adding a1 and b1, excel updates the sum automatically when you change the values in one of those cells.

Try using this approach to do different forms of arithmetics on the other numbers in columns a and b.

Unlock the strength of functions

The greatest strength of excel lies in functions. Those let you use a couple of keypresses to run complex calculations.

We're only barely going to scratch the feature surface here.

Most formulas take sets of numbers and give you information.

Average function, for example, gives you an average set of numbers. Let's just try to use it.

Select the empty cell, and type the formula below:

= Mean(a1: a4)

Then hit enter.

	A	B	C	D
1	13	37	0.25	
2	21	4		
3	-34	17		
4	1	0		
5	Welcome to	Spreadsheeto		
6				
7				
8				

The resulting number, 0.25, represents the average number in cells a1, a2, a3, and a4.

Notation of cell ranges

In the above formula, we used "a1: a4" to tell Excel to look at all the cells between a1 and a4, including those two. You could read it as "a1 by a4."

You may also do it to have numbers in different columns. 'A5: c7' means a5, a6, a7, b5, b6, b7, c5, c6, and c7.

Some roles operate on a text as well.

Let's just try this concatenate feature!

Select and type this formula into cell c5:

= Concatenate(a5,, "b5)

Then hit enter.

In the cell, you will see the "welcome to spreadsheeto" post.

How did they do this? Concatenate takes and places cells with text in them.

We put together the contents of both a5 and b5. However, because we still wanted space between "to" and "spreadsheeto," a third claim was included: the space between two quotes.

You can combine cell references (such as "a5″) and typed values (such as" ") into formulas.

Excel has hundreds of functional apps. To find the function that solves a particular problem, go to the Formulas tab and click on one of the icons:

Scroll through the feature list and pick the one you want (you may have to look around for a while).

So excel lets you achieve the right numbers in the right places:

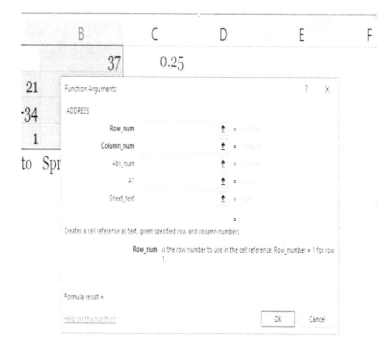

If you start typing a formula, beginning with the equals symbol, excel will support you by showing you some possible features you may want:

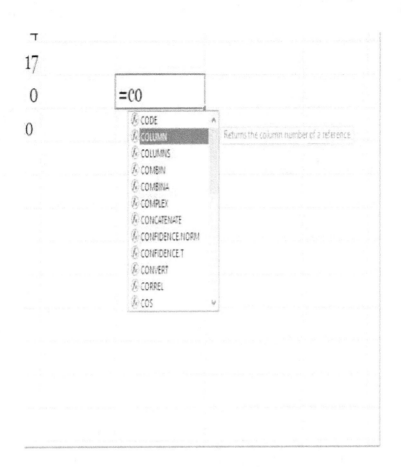

And finally, after the name of the formula and the opening parenthesis have been written, excel will tell you the arguments you need to go where:

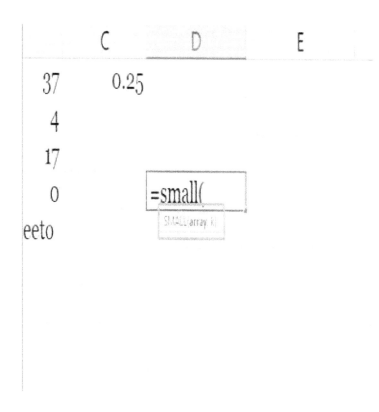

If you've never used a feature before, Excel's reminders may be difficult to understand. But that's going to become obvious as you get more practice.

Here is a tiny preview of how and what roles can operate. It should be enough to get you to carry out the tasks you need to do immediately.

Saving your job and sharing it

You would want to save your changes after you've done a lot of work on your spreadsheet.

To save, press Ctrl+s. When you haven't saved your file yet, you'll be told where to save it and what to call it.

You can also press the Save button in the toolbar for easy access:

Getting into the habit of saving always is a good idea.
It's a hassle to try to restore unsaved adjustments!

The best way to distribute the spreadsheets is via one drive.

Click the Share button in the window's top-right corner, and Excel will guide you through your document sharing.

You can also save the document and e-mail it, or share it with others through some other cloud service.

USEFUL EXCELLENT SHORTCUTS THAT FACILITATE YOUR WORK

Excel is one of the most commonly used tabular data management and manipulation software. If you've come to this site, I presume you're an avid user of this software and need some excellent shortcuts to make your work easier. Keep on!

Excellent shortcuts: next working manual or previous workbook

The shortcut for opening the next workbook is ctrl + tab, both for windows and mac. You will click Ctrl + Shift + tab to open the previous workbook.

Great shortcuts: Current workbook or previous workbook

We have to switch between different worksheets in the same workbook several times. The shortcut to this mission comes handy and makes it much easier to work!

Shortcut to step straight onto the next sheet:

For Windows: pgdn + ctrl

For Mac: Fn + Ctrl + Arrow down

Shortcut to move left onto the next sheet:

For Windows: PgUp + ctrl

For mac: fn + ctrl + ft up

Great shortcuts: anything to choose from

Ctrl + a is a shortcut to the "select all" features. Nevertheless, in excel, this shortcut behaves differently in various ways.

In case the cursor is in a void cell, ctrl + a selects the entire worksheet. In any case, if the cursor is in a set of bordering cells, ctrl + a will pick the entire collection of cells.

This ctrl + a action is different when the cursor is in a line. When you first use ctrl + a, you select only the table data. If you use Ctrl + A again, you can also select the table header along with the table info. For the 3rd time, the entire Excel worksheet will be picked by using ctrl+ a continuously.

Excellent shortcuts in the present worksheet: go to the first cell

Exploration of larger worksheets can become completely monotonous. You may also use the scroll bars to look at the worksheet, but using the scroll bars takes a great deal of patience. If you want to enter the very first cell, that is the current worksheet a1 cell, use the shortcut below:

For Windows: home + ctrl

For mac: fn + left arrow + ctrl

This shortcut will take you directly to the a1 cell, regardless of your current location on the worksheet!

Great shortcuts: go to the final cell in the existing worksheet

The first question in your mind could arise — what's the last cell in a worksheet?

The last cell in the worksheet is at the last column crossing point containing information, and the last row containing information. It can happen several times that the last cell of the worksheet has no data in it.

Shortcut to the final cell in the worksheet:

Ctrl + end for windows

For mac: fn + right arrow ctrl + right

One of the functions of this shortcut is to check quickly if there are any data in the sheet you don't know about. There might be some stray data in the worksheet in a very distant cell. This shortcut comes to rescue and will allow you to test it. After all, if you'd like to print your data in the worksheet, you don't want to print 20 blank pages just to find any stray data in some distant cell!

Excel shortcuts: pick a row in the current worksheet or column

Some of the most common tasks in Excel is to pick a row or a column. Fortunately for that, there are shortcuts too!

Excellent shortcut for choosing a row: Shift + space

Excel column shortcut: ctrl + room

If the desired row or column is selected, you can expand the selection by keeping the shift key along with the correct arrow key.

Excellent shortcuts: ribbon extension, or collapse

If you do not need it, you could remove the ribbon and put it back if and when you like, using the shortcuts below.

Windows shortcuts: ctrl + f1

Mac shortcuts: order + choice + r

Excellent shortcuts: A set of non-adjacent cells

Many of the can tasks we do on excel include the selection of non-adjacent cells. You may want to insert the same data in the selected non-adjacent cells, remove their data, etc. Non-adjacent cells can be conveniently selected using Ctrl + Windows click and + Mac click command. You need to pick the first cell and then hold the ctrl or command key when clicking on other cells in our list.

Excellent shortcuts: pick till the data edge

Exploring large tables (say, containing 15,000 rows) at high speeds is enjoyable, but to do so, you will need to pick large groups of cells. If you're going to have to do this manually, it's likely to take you a long time. Quite long, actually.

You can use the following shortcuts to avoid scrolling and still pick to the edge of the data:

Right search shortcut: Shift + Ctrl + right arrow

Link selection shortcut: Shift + Ctrl + left arrow

Upward range shortcut: Move + Ctrl + Up arrow

Shortcut to pick downward: move + ctrl + down arrow

Even if the cursor is going fast, don't worry, the selection will be precise.

Shortcuts excellent: find next match

Seeing a piece of text is one of the most frequently performed tasks on any data-processing program. To use the Excel find function, you can use the shortcuts below:

For Windows: f + ctrl

For mac: the + f command

You can keep looking for subsequent matches until you've found at least one match, using Shift + f4 on windows and command + g on mac.

Excellent shortcuts: view of the active cell on the current worksheet

Our cursor gets lost several times and is nowhere in sight. In such a case, you can use ctrl + backspace on windows and command + delete on mac to put the cursor back in view. In the worksheet, you'll find the cursor beautifully focused.

Excellent shortcuts: add a new line inside the current cell

The shortcuts below will allow you to reach new lines inside the current cell:

For windows join alt +

For mac: Control + Return option

Excellent shortcuts: insert current date or time of day

Shortcuts will often come handy for entering the current date or time. You will be able to do these things easily by taking shortcuts.

Present date shortcut: search +;

Shortcut for determining current time: power + move +:

Excellent shortcuts: red, Italic, focus

Formatting words to make them look bold, italic, or highlighted is one of the activities most commonly performed in excel. The relevant text will, after all, stand out from the usual text to underline its significance!

In browsers, shortcut for "bold": ctrl + b

Shortcut in mac to "bold": + b command

"Italic" shortcut on windows: ctrl + I

Make the "italic" shortcut in mac: command + I

Windows shortcut for 'underline': ctrl + u

Create "underline" shortcut in mac: + u order

Excellent shortcuts: insert columns or rows into a table

You need to pick a whole row or column first to insert a row or column using an Excel shortcut. Include a new row adjacent to the selected row or add a new column to the right of the selected column using the shortcut Ctrl + Shift + + in windows (and control + I in mac).

Use the same shortcut to insert several rows or columns, too. To do so, you must pick the number of rows or columns equal to the number of new rows or columns that you wish to insert.

Great shortcuts: delete the columns or rows in a table

To delete a single row or column, pick it and use the + - (works for both Windows and Mac) shortcut. You can also delete several rows or columns by choosing all of them using the same shortcut.

The shortcuts above are really useful when you're working with excel. I hope you've found them helpful and always use them. Enjoy super easy-working!

Microsoft Excel is a popular spreadsheet software program and a fairly old one; the first version appeared as early as 1984. Each new version of Excel came with more and more new shortcuts, and you may feel a little surprised to see the full list (over 200!). Don't worry, anyway! For daily work, 20 or 30 keyboard shortcuts would be completely sufficient, while others are intended for highly specialized tasks such as writing VBA macros, outlining details, managing pivot tables, recalculating large workbooks, etc.

I have put together a list of the most popular shortcuts below, and you can download it for convenience as a printable image (shortcuts-page1, shortcuts-page2) or as a pdf-file.

You can download the original workbook if you want to rearrange the shortcuts to your taste or expand the list.

No workbook can do without excellent shortcuts.

I know these are simple shortcuts, and most of you are at ease with them. Still, let me write them down for starters again.

Note for newbies: The plus sign "+" means that the keys should be pressed at the same time. At the bottom left and bottom right of most keyboards are the ctrl and alt buttons.

Ctrl over n

Build a whole new workbook.

Click to + o

Open the latest workbook.

Strg + s

Save Workbook Live.

F12-F12

Save the active workbook with a new name, save as a dialogue box.

W + Ctrl

Close the Workbook.

Ctrl over c

Copy the selected cell contents to the clipboard.

Ctrl + x Command

Cut the selected cell contents to a clipboard.

Ctrl + rev

Insert the clipboard contents into the cell(s) you picked.

Ctrl + to z

Undo the last step. Taste Panic:)

P + Ctrl

Open the dialogue on "Write."

Data Formatting

Ctrl + One

Open a dialogue called the "type cells."

Ctrl over t

"Convert selected cells into a table. You can also pick any cell within a range of relevant data, and pressing ctrl+t will create a table.

Find out more about Tables Excel and its functionality.

Operated to formulae

Tabula

Example: enter = and start typing vl, click on the tab and you will get = vlookup)

f4

Put the cursor within a cell and hit f4 to get the correct reference type: absolute, relative, or mixed (relative column and absolute line, absolute column, and relative line).

Ctrl + Alt +

Toggle between the cell values and formulas shown.

Ctrl + Alt +

Insert the above cell formula into the cell currently selected, or the formula circle.

Data navigation and visualization

Ctrl + and f1

Show/hide the ribbon Excel. Show the ribbon to display over four rows of details.

Page ctrl +

Turn to Excel Workbook next available.

Ctrl + Scroll down

Switch to the next worksheet. To return to the previous one, click ctrl + PgUp.

Trash + g

Open the dialogue called "go to." Pressing f5 will show the same dialogue.

Click over f

Show the dialogue box, "To search."

Homestay

Switch to current row 1st cell in the worksheet.

Ctrl + home mode

Moving to worksheet start (a1 cell).

Click + Exit

Shift to the last used cell in the current worksheet, i.e., the lowest column row at the top.

Output data

f2

Edit the cell you are actually in.

Alt + Fill in

Type a new line (carriage return) into a cell in cell editing mode.

Ctrl + Ctrl;

Enter the current date. To enter the current time, press Ctrl + Shift +;

Enter Ctrl +

Fill the contents of the current cell into the selected cells.

Example: select several cells. Press and hold down ctrl, click any selected cell, and press f2 to edit it. Then hit ctrl + enter and copy the contents of the edited cell to all selected cells.

Ctrl plus d

Copy the first cell contents and position within the specified range into the cells below. If more than one column is chosen, the top cell contents of each column will be copied downwards.

Click + Switch + V

When the clipboard is not clean, open the "paste special" window.

Ctrl + and

If possible, repeat (redo) the last move.

Choosing Information

Alt + Alt

Pick the entire worksheet. If the cursor is already within a list, click once to pick the list, press one more time to select the entire worksheet.

Ctrl + home and then ctrl + turn + end

In the current worksheet, pick the full range of your actual user data.

Click + Floor

Select the complete board.

Shift + Range

Select the full list.

HOW TO DEEPLY ANALYZE THE DATA, FILTER AND SORT DATA

If you have thousands of rows stored in the Excel 2019 spreadsheet, it is difficult to recognize data, particularly if you try to locate rows that suit a particular requirement or definition. Excel has the option of sorting and filtering data to either set up a data table in a specific order or use formatting to make certain data stand out.

Server configuration

When sorting and conditionally formatting data, it's usually a large number of rows. The following examples use a set of 20 rows of data. The data reflects a list of customers and the sum of revenue produced by each transaction.

(Sorting and formatting examples of data setups)

Note that headers are used at the top of each column. It is useful for sorting when you decide to adjust the column to sort on. Excel's sorting feature is helpful even though you only have a few rows. When you need to display a list of revenue numbers based on the highest value or the lowest value, instead of analyzing values and deciding the right one based on your own human analysis, Excel 2019 will do so.

Sorting out details

Excel provides a few options for sorting data. First, you can sort one column of data with just a click of a button. To assign an order to a single column, select the column by clicking the letter label at the top. Excel gives you two buttons to sort either by ascending or descending values of the column selected.

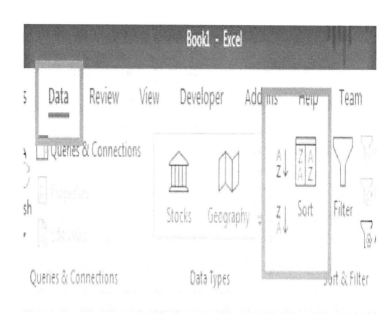

(Buttons for Type Excel)

Two buttons to the left of the "sort" button shown in the above image. You can also sort a specified range of cells and order only specified data. Copy and paste a small portion of the test data to a different column. Highlight only those cells and then press the sort order you want to set for the selected range.

The button showing an arrow pointing down, with the first letting being a will sort ascending values. The button that shows a pointing arrow where the first letter is z will sort values in downward order.

Excel should be able to determine whether the data is a series of dates, text values, or numbers. The sort function then commands cells based on the type of data that is detected. If you have got a list of revenue sales, for example, excel knows how to sort cells based on numerical values. When you have cells formatted as dates, excel knows that the chronological order of these values should be set. Cells, which are text values like customer names, are ordered in alphabetical order.

We have two columns to sort because we have a list of customers and their income. If you are using the Single-Column Sort keys, order one column, and your data will be corrupted. This problem is solved by the "sort" button by offering a way to hold the columns linked while sorting data depending on the column you choose to use for the sort.

The first move is to locate the cells in our row. Make sure you include the headers in the column since excel uses them as part of the sorting feature. Click the "type" button, and asking for feedback opens a window.

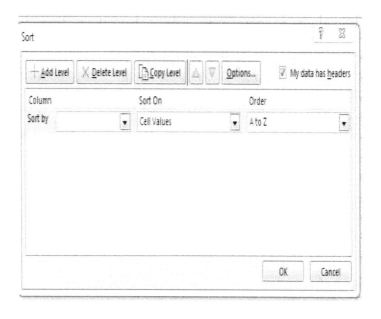

(Sort the Setup window)

The drop-down "order by" has the headers indicated for every column. Since we have both "customer" and "revenue" as headers for columns, these two values are shown in the drop-down "order by." If you do not have headers for the columns, excel lists the labels for the column letters. If you have multiple columns, having only letter labels will make configuring your sort order difficult.

The "type on" drop-down defaults to "cell values," which means the value for the form will be used. These are the standard configurations, but you can also sort by the color of the cell or font. This is useful when setting conditional formatting, which is covered in the following section.

The drop-down "order" indicates whether you wish to sort data in ascending or descending order. The choice "a to z" means you want to sort data in ascending order. The "z to a" choice means you want the data to be ordered in descending order.

Let's sort on the "revenue" column in this case, and leave the other drop-down options set to normal. Click the "ok" button to sort the data.

B21	⋮	×	✓	*fx*	7657

	A	B	C	D
1	**Customer**	**Revenue**		
2	Jacob	$ 12.00		
3	Maci	$ 13.00		
4	Kim	$ 24.00		
5	Brad	$ 44.00		
6	Sally	$ 63.00		
7	William	$ 76.00		
8	Christine	$ 86.00		
9	Mark	$ 123.00		
10	John	$ 234.00		
11	Michelle	$ 324.00		
12	Joe	$ 324.00		
13	Greg	$ 345.00		
14	Toby	$ 432.00		
15	Ethel	$ 432.00		
16	Rick	$ 555.00		
17	Brittany	$ 656.00		
18	Jennifer	$ 765.00		
19	Kelly	$5,423.00		
20	Tyler	$7,345.00		
21	Eric	$7,657.00		
22				
23				

(Sorted by "income")

Please notice that names also match revenue values. This is because the "sort" feature is capable of keeping the rows aligned even though you order data by one column. If you want to change the customer names order, repeat those steps, and pick "customer" from the drop-down "filter by." Columns are still correctly spaced, but rows are arranged again, depending on the name of the consumer.

CONDITIONAL DELIVEMENT

Data sorting does not highlight certain cells that may need to stand out amongst others. You would want to know, for example, which customers had sales within a certain range. You may want to know which customers had income below or above a specified threshold. All of your records can be sifted, but conditional formatting that changes the font or background makes these cells stand out much more and make them easier to find. You can quickly identify the customers who purchased and contributed revenue to your profits with a short customer revenue list that includes only 20 rows, but if you had thousands of records, such a sorted list would make it difficult to locate individual records.

Excel has a "conditional formatting" feature that adjusts the color of a cell's font or a cell's background color to make it stand out and easy to find when you're searching for certain values that fulfill a condition.

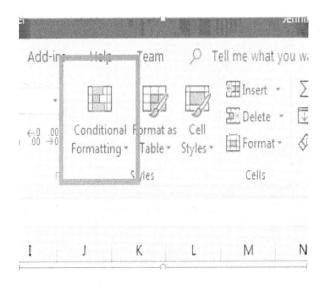

(Conditional Click on Formatting)

The button "Conditional Formatting" can be found in the ribbon tab "Home." The above picture shows the conditional formatting button, which is also in the category "types."

Before you set conditional formatting, pick only the currency cells. If you highlight all the cells, including customer names, exc 2019 will not be able to differentiate text from currency values and will not highlight the right cells. When you click on the button, a drop-down list contains many choices.

(Conditional Drop-down Options to Format)

As you can see from the above picture, conditional formatting offers you various options. The most widely used feature is "highlight cell rules," which also has many choices if you click on them. These choices are good for numeric values when you want to differentiate those cells, among others. You can choose between greater than smaller than and equal to. These options help you to find customer sales based on the amount of money that they brought in according to the spreadsheet.

You aren't limited to only one color with one condition with conditional formatting. Using different conditions, you can set several colors. You would want to know, for example, which customers brought in sales under $100 and which customers brought in more than $1000. You can then take the data and use it for reporting and information about the product. You know then which customers are the best (or worst) to market and upsell additional products, using revenue charts and conditional formatting.

We want to know, in this case, the customers brought in revenue over $1000. Again, by looking at the twenty records with rows sorted in descending order using the sort function, you can see this information. But imagine of a spreadsheet with thousands of records, and how hard it would be to find all customers even if those rows are sorted in ascending or downward order.

From the drop-down options for "highlight cells rules," pick the "greater than" option. This opens a new settings window.

(Greater Window than Conditional Formatting Setup)

Notice a value is filled in automatically. This default value lets you set your conditional formatting to a midpoint, but you'll probably need to change this setting on your own. We want to know which values are higher than $1000, so enter 1000 in the text box for the input value. You can also pick one cell to be your configuration value if you press the up arrow.

As you change the value in the text box input, exc 2019 will display the cells that will change in your selected group of cells if you press the "ok" button. When pressing the up arrow button, press "enter" after a value has been selected, or enter a value in the text box input, and click "enter."

The next drop-down lists both the history of a cell and its font colors. The default is a light red (pink) color filling with a darker red font. You may also opt to change just the background color, or only change the font color. To see a list of choices and colors, press the drop-down. We will use the default option in this example, and change the color of both the background of the cell and the foreground font.

To view results in your spreadsheet, click the "ok" button.

	A	B	C
1	Customer	Revenue	
2	Jacob	$ 12.00	
3	Maci	$ 13.00	
4	Kim	$ 24.00	
5	Brad	$ 44.00	
6	Sally	$ 63.00	
7	William	$ 76.00	
8	Christine	$ 86.00	
9	Mark	$ 123.00	
10	John	$ 234.00	
11	Michelle	$ 324.00	
12	Joe	$ 324.00	
13	Greg	$ 345.00	
14	Toby	$ 432.00	
15	Ethel	$ 432.00	
16	Rick	$ 555.00	
17	Brittany	$ 656.00	
18	Jennifer	$ 765.00	
19	Kelly	$ 5,423.00	
20	Tyler	$ 7,345.00	
21	Eric	$ 7,657.00	
22			

(Conditional on-cell formatting package greater than $1000)

You can now quickly see, with conditional formatting, which customers brought in revenue over $1000. This formatting continues even when you use the "sort" method to sort the cells again. If you want to use certain conditions, you should give them different colors so you can easily differentiate between the two conditions.

One reason why many businesses use excel 2019 is due to the many options that are available when charting and sorting the data. Sorting data makes an easy analysis of the data much easier, and you can also make it easier for other users to find information when they are not familiar with the data. Conditional formatting offers an additional aesthetic touch, particularly when you have thousands of records to review. Conditional formatting can save hours in charting and reviewing time for anyone who needs to look at numbers in a spreadsheet for 2019 excel.

When you understand how conditional formatting and sorting works, you can find it much easier to work with large data sets, especially revenue sheets, that need to be evaluated every month.

CREATING PIVOT TABLES AND CHARTS AGAINST YOUR DATE

For those of you have followed my work for the past decade (or more), you know the long period between 2008 (when this was originally penned) and today,

not a great deal of excel time between 2008 (when this was originally penned)

The result, this sort of a rankings distribution chart: a pivot table in excel and how to construct a pivot chart with the data:

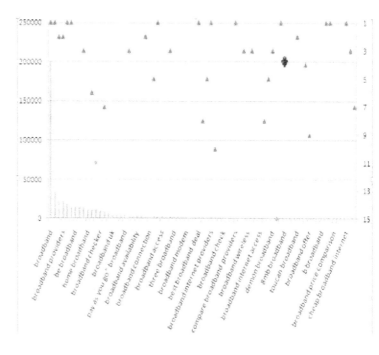

The chart above displays search volume and ranking position in google on the secondary axis. It was my favorite form of SEO chart of the day.

Back then, we used google keyword tool data, and rankings gathered from awr studies. Today, it's a little different. We're going to catch data from the semrush API.

Should you have to use a separate source of ranking data, or you might need to use vlookup to consolidate your information table in this single table? Follow the links provided and the final data set.

Here's to create a pivot table in excel:

Gather info.

To offer a table.

Head to insert > pivot table then and a new sheet

Attach axis fields, values, filters, labels, columns.

Add filters substantial dragging fields into 'filters.'

Use sort to arrange your table in whatever want you ord.

I way take the process step on my Excel 365 installation. The cycle will be more or less 2013, 2016 and 2019.

Table to your data and build a master

Pull down all keyword knowledge using your analysis weapon of choice. Today, we use semrush. Here's the animated gif of the method i used with seo tools for excel and the SEMRUSH API:

Use SEO tools to excel, through the SEMRUSH API.

But i like really to. Amongst other factors, tables seem to be highly performant, less work for you in this particular use case, and they can fun to the name.

Make a table by selecting the dataset in its entirety (ctrl+shift+down then right), then ctrl+l generates the list:

Name the table unforgettable, including "rankings."

Build a pivot table on a new sheet

Now we have all of your data nicely arranged in one place, let's get to the fun part. We go to shift a pivot table to a new board.

Just like this:

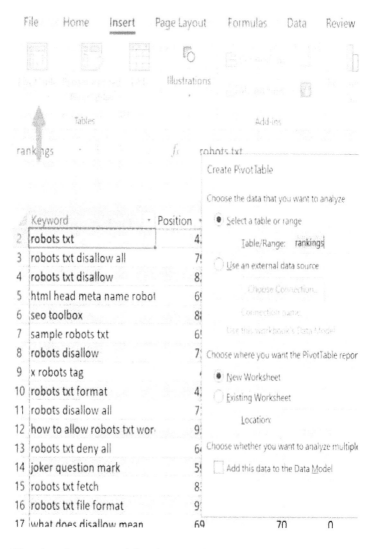

Illustrations

Tables   Add-ins

rankings f_c robots.txt

Create PivotTable

Choose the data that you want to analyze

	Keyword	Position
2	robots txt	4:
3	robots txt disallow all	7!
4	robots txt disallow	8:
5	html head meta name robot	6!
6	seo toolbox	8!
7	sample robots txt	6!
8	robots disallow	7:
9	x robots tag	
10	robots txt format	4:
11	robots disallow all	7:
12	how to allow robots txt wor	9:
13	robots txt deny all	6:
14	joker question mark	5!
15	robots txt fetch	8:
16	robots txt file format	9:
17	what does disallow mean	69

● Select a table or range

   Table/Range: rankings

○ Use an external data source

   Choose Connection...

   Connection name:

   Use this workbook's Data Model

Choose where you want the PivotTable repor

● New Worksheet

○ Existing Worksheet

   Location:

Choose whether you want to analyze multiple

☐ Add this data to the Data Model

                 70   0

Head to insert > table pivot and a new sheet

when you press "yes," with a blank pivot table "land list" and a pivot map "filter window" on the right of your screen and a pivottable on the left 'pivottable1'

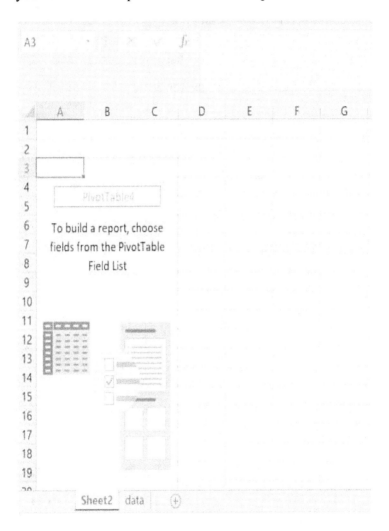

Add axis fields, values, column labels, and filters

If you're new to pivot charts, you're about to experience a bit of a penny drop moment. If you're new to pivot charts, you're about to experience a bit of a penny drop moment.

The pivottable field list uses drag and drop functionality to popular the little white squares with values.

Start by picking up your keywords table, the keyword tab. Next, drag and drop your question figure at the "values" tab.

Your table on the left will start of sense: looking at 'amount of search volume' and not 'count of search volume.'

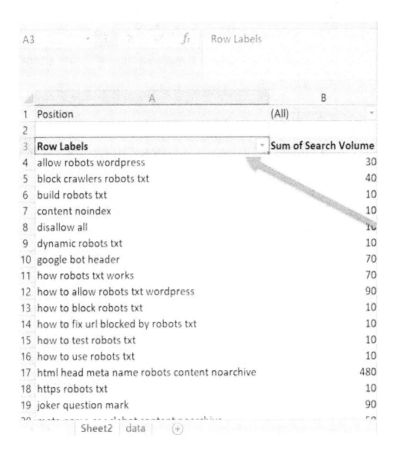

	A	B
A3	f_x Row Labels	
1	Position	(All)
2		
3	Row Labels	Sum of Search Volume
4	allow robots wordpress	30
5	block crawlers robots txt	40
6	build robots txt	10
7	content noindex	10
8	disallow all	10
9	dynamic robots txt	10
10	google bot header	70
11	how robots txt works	70
12	how to allow robots txt wordpress	90
13	how to block robots txt	10
14	how to fix url blocked by robots txt	10
15	how to test robots txt	10
16	how to use robots txt	10
17	html head meta name robots content noarchive	480
18	https robots txt	10
19	joker question mark	90

Sheet2 | data | (+)

You'll very quickly find that you've built thing a beauty.

A pivot table with all keywords in your list and all search volume values corresponding to them.

This is what I call pivot-table-penny-drop-moment. Nonetheless, putting all your values in a pivot table may not be what you expected, which is where the filters join.

I dragged the "location" field into "filters," as you can see. This adds a helpful drop over the pivot table, which I can use to filter out the very low volume search values.

To build a filter, follow the yellow arrow (in the screenshot above) to the drop-down filter and check the checkbox "Pick multiple objects." You now have the option of clearing any unnecessary data from your list, in my case, low search volume.

Finally, move the "location" values to "values," and you will have a pivot table with keywords, search volume, and chart rankings.

Build pivot diagram

To attach your map, head to Attach > column or bar line. Nonetheless, it can look a little rough around the edges, so let's make it look a lot better than this:

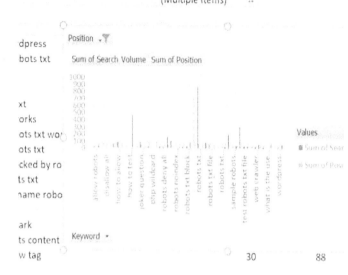

First, by search volume, we need to arrange keywords so that we can look at our map as a tail graph. Highlight the search volume data (the column you want to sort in the order of the volume) and pick "data > sort."

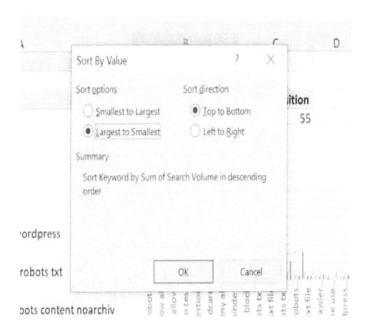

This will marginally improve matters, but the map may contain a few too many keywords. Try filtering out the words of the smaller number, at least for now.

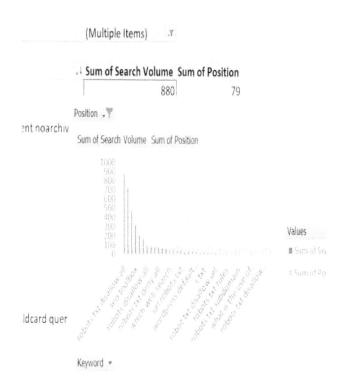

Filter the ranks by keyword

The only remaining challenge is to arrange the rankings in a way that makes sense visually.

You can never simply equate various types of values on the same chart axis, so let's create a secondary rating axis.

Next, choosing and editing data series rankings. You might use the right mouse button on the map to pick "data series format," but that's fiddly and unnecessary.

Choose your chart instead, and navigate to the "format" pane.

Looking for a "current selection" drop-down to the far left of the screen. Select Drop-down and press the data sequence of your rankings, now choose "Collection format."

The data will be put on the secondary axis, and the chart form will be modified to a line map. Finally, we must remove the lines in the rating chart so that only the markers are left.

Dealing with the secondary axis and changing the form of a diagram

By default, the pivot diagram shows both data series as bar charts. We need to pick our series again (using the drop-down format selection), then right-click the "Change series chart sort" button.

From the options in this dialogue, select "Custom" and choose the stacked line option for your secondary axis:

These pivot charts use a secondary reversed axis to place one ranking at the top of the chart.

We would need to change the secondary axis to be able to do so.

Right-click on your chart 's secondary axis and select "format axis" Setting your minimum rating to "1.0" eliminates all zeroes in the data in your rankings and setting a limit of say, 15 will exclude any ranking above 15. You decide which selection is best for you.

Finally, scrolling down those options shows a checkbox: click "Reverse Order Values," and you're almost done.

Last touches

One small point left to do; we can adjust the form of the chart, so our secondary data makes a little more sense.

Select data bar rankings and navigate to "Project > Switch Diagram Form" Use line graph option with visible line data markers. Delete the color line from the inside of "Data Series Format > Line Color," and you're done.

METHODS OF USING EXCEL 2019: CREATING BUDGET PLANS AND CALCULATING ALL TYPES OF PAYMENTS

If you have never opened your office suite spreadsheet, you 're missing out on a really useful program. Here's how to create a household budget using it.

All office suites have a spreadsheet, but this must be one of the least-used apps of all of them-not least because what you can do with it is far from apparent. Here, then, is a starting guide for anyone who wants to make some use of their spreadsheet.

We create a basic budget for households that you can use to keep track of monthly incomes and outgoings. You can use this sort of sheet to figure out how much you can save on an expensive purchase, for example, and add some simple sheet principles that you can apply to other items.

We used excel here, but in any spreadsheet program, the steps should be more or less the same.

Step 1: establish some headings in the row

Start your application with a spreadsheet and create a new, blank sheet. We shall begin by listing the outgoing forms in columns a and b. In corresponding cells form the following:

A2: Expenditures

A3: Tickets

A8: Audi Q5

A11: Recreational

A13: Meals & Drinks

A15: Miscarriage

A16: Average

A18: Earnings

A20: Net Wire

Step 2: establish certain categories

Now switch to cell b3 and type the corresponding cells into the following:

B3: Recruit

B4: Oil-Gas

B5: The power market

B6: vapor velocities

B7: Revenue by council

B8: Fuel

B9: An insurance scheme

B10: Highway levy

B11: license tv

B12: Full team

B13: Lebensmittelgeschäfte

B14: Takeovers

B15: Inm.

B18: Wages

B20: Close net

This provided a clear list of outgoings and incomes, grouped into groups — feel free to change them if they do not suit your circumstances in particular.

Step 3: create monthly column headings.

Finally, type Jan in cell c2 and start with Feb, Mar, and so on through the rest of the row until you get to n2 to build 12 months of column headers.

Stage 4: Enter the one-month figures

Now to enter some monthly outgoings and income estimates, beginning with the Jan column. Again, it's easier to copy our figures here, but do not hesitate to use your own, particularly if you've changed the categories in columns a and b.

Phase 5: apply gross expenses

Now for the overall cost to sort out. Please select c16 and type:

= (c3: c15)

... And click back key. It is known as the 'formula' in the spreadsheet parlance, and the opening = sign informs excel that the equation must be done using the following. The number is the actual formula and, in this case, applies the range of cells in brackets-c3 to c15, inclusive.

Step 6: work out earnings minus output

Type your salary into cell c18, and we can now work out how much money is left at the end of the month. It is a much simpler formula that only eliminates the total revenue production, so type the following in cell c20:

= 18–c16

Phase 7: Copy figures from one month

Rather of inserting more figures into the Feb (d) to Dec (n) columns, copying and pasting the Jan (c) column is easier. Click on cell c3 and drag down the mouse to cell c20 to pick all the figures. Press the keyboard shortcut Ctrl + c to copy. The selected set of cells is now outlined with a dotted blinking outline.

Stage 8: paste the figures onto the remaining sheet

Now pick the selection of Jan column cells to paste to. Select cell d3, and move the mouse to cell n20 just as before. Click [ctrl] + [v] keyboard shortcut to paste the copied cells in step 7.

Excel should use some knowledge to paste the cells here and update some formulas to keep them stable. We then added quarterly gas and electricity payments in columns sea, Jun, Sep, and Dec to our example.

Stage 9: Change the net monthly formulae

The only issue now is that the formulas in row 20 (net) do not take into account the balance of the previous month, so we will have to make a small adjustment. Choose d20 cell and type:

= d18-d16+c20 Take

This will delete the current cell contents and add the net Jan figure to the net Feb figure. You can now copy cell d20 and paste it into cells e20 through n20 using the same technique as phase 8.

Stage 10: Plate shape

The final step is to format a table sheet to make it more understandable. For our example, we made the row (row 2) and column (a and b) headings bold, along with the rows for gross, net, and profit. We also added a certain color and alignment and formatted all figures as currencies.

We'll let you find out how to do this — just pick the cell ranges you want to format and use the home tab formatting options if you're using Excel. You may also need to adjust the column widths to fit the contents — just drag the dividing line between the headers of each column (a, b, etc.) to do this.

USING FUNCTIONS AND FORMULAS LIKE IF, DATE, DATEDIF, LEN, MID, AND VLOOKUP

Date and Time Works

Excel offers other features for dates and times to work with.

Now and aujourd'hui

You will get the latest date with the function today, and the new date and time with the function now. Technically, the function now returns the current date and time, but as shown below, you can format only as time:

Today) (/ returns actual date

Now) (/ returns real-time

Note: these functions are unpredictable and will be recalculated with any shift in the worksheet. When you want a static value, use the shortcuts on date and time.

Day, month, year, date;

You can use the functions of day, month and year to disassemble each date into its raw components, and the date feature to bring it back together.

= date('14-November-2018) '/ returns 14

= Month('14-November 2018)) '/ returns 11

= Year('14-Nov-2018) '/ 2018 returns

= Date(2018,11,14) / 14-Nov-2018 returns

Day, hour, minute, second.

Excel includes a set of functions for parallel periods. You could use the hr, minute, and second functions to extract time pieces, and you can assemble time with the time function from individual components.

= time('10:30) "/ returns 10

Returns 30 = minute("10:30) "/

=('10:30") / returns 0

Returns = time(10,30,0)/ 10:30

Date and Year Pause

You can use the datedif feature to get time in years, months, or days between dates. In "normalized" denominations, that is, "2 yrs and 5 months and 27 days," datedif can also be configured to get the total time.

To get fractional years, using yearfrac:

= Yearfrac("14-November-2018,"10-Jun-2021")/ returns 2.57

Edited and revised

Shifting the date forward (or backward) by a specified number of months is a common task for dates. For that, you can use the functions edate and eomonth. Moves by month edate and maintains the day. Eomonth operates the same way but returns on the last day of the month.

Edate(date,6) / 6 months notice

Eomonth(date,6)/ 6 months in advance (end of month)

Working hours and networking days

You may use the working-day feature to find out a date n working days in the future. You may use the Networkdays to measure the number of working days between two dates.

Working days (start, n, holidays) / Date n future workdays

Networkdays(starting, finishing, vacations) / number of working days between dates

Note: both functions will automatically skip weekends (Saturday and Sunday) and, if given, skip holidays too. If you want more flexibility on what days the weekends are considered, see workday. Intl and network days.intl feature.

Weekdays and Weekends

Excel offers the weekday feature to find out the day of the week from a date. Returns a weekday number from 1-7 showing Sunday, Monday, Tuesday, etc. to use the weeknum feature to get the week number in the year.

= Date of the week/returns the number 1-7

= week num(date)/returns the number of the week in year

Ingeniery

Conversion

Most engineering functions are very technical. You'll find plenty of functions in this section for complex numbers. Convert feature is therefore very useful for daily conversions of units. You can use convert units to adjust distance, weight, temperature, and more.

Returns 22.2 = convert(72,"f","c")/

Functions of information

Isblank, lake, and isformula

Excel offers multiple cell value test functions, including isumber, istext, islogical, isblank, and isformula, also called "is" functions, and all return true or false based on cell content.

Excel also has isodd functions, and iseven is checking a no. To know if it is even or not.

Logical Features

Logical functions in Excel are the main building block in many advanced formulae. Logical functions return true or false Boolean values. If you need a rational formula primordial, this video will go through several examples.

And, or, not

The essence of the logical functions of Excel is the function and function, the function or process, and not the process. Both of these functions will be used in the screen below to run a simple test on the values in column b:

= & (b5>3,b5<9)

= and(b5=3,b5=9)

= and not(b5=2)

Iferror, or ifna

The iferror and ifna function can be used to capture and manage errors in a simple manner. Vlookup is used to access costs from a menu object on the screen below. Column f contains only a vlookup feature, without handling any errors. Column g depicts how to use ifna with vlookup to display a custom message when entering a non-recognized object.

= vlookup(e5,menu,2,0)/ No trapping of errors

Catch errors = ifna(vlookup(e5,menu,2,0),"not found) "/

Whereas ifna just catches a # n / a error, iferror can catch any error on the formula.

If functions and ifs

If function is one of the functions most used in Excel. If test scores are reviewed in the screen below, and "pass" or "fail" is assigned:

Many as functions can be clustered to perform more complex logical tests together.

The ifs function could run multiple logical tests without nesting ifs in excel through office 365.

=

ifs(c5<60,"f,"c5<70,"d,"c5<80,"c,"c5,c5<90,"b,"c5>90,"a)

Lookup functions and search functions

Vlookup and icing on

Excel provides a range of search and data retrieval features. Vlookup is most popular of all:

= vlookup(c5,f5:g7,2,Really)

Hlookup functions like vlookup, but requires horizontally organized data to:

= Hlookup(c5,g4:i5,2,Really)

Indice and match

Index and match provide more versatility and power for more complicated lookups:

= Index(C5:E12, match h4,b5:b12,0)(h5,c4: e4,0))

Both the index funand the match function are powerful functions that appear in formulae of all kinds.

Lookout

The default behaviors in the lookup feature make it useful when solving other issues.

Lookup assumes that values are sorted in ascending order, and the approximate match is always finished. If lookup can not find a match, the next smallest value will suit. For the example below, we use the Lookup to find the last column entry:

Row & Column

The row function and column function can be used to locate row and column numbers on a worksheet. Note the return values for the current cell in both row and column, if no reference is provided:

The row function often shows up in advanced formulas processing data with relative row numbers.

Bars & Columns

The function of the rows and columns gives the number of rows in a relation. In the screen below, we list rows and columns in a table of excel called "Table1."

Note rows returns the number of rows of data in a list, excluding the header line. By the way, there are 23 things to learn about Tables Excel.

Hyperlinking

You may use the hyperlink feature to link to a formula. Note hyperlink lets you build external links as well as internal links:

= Relink(c5,b5)

Tripoddata

Getpivotdata is a valuable feature for extracting information from current pivot tables.

= Getpivotdata(sales,b4,"region, i6,"product",i7)

Select

The select feature is useful anytime you need to make a number-based choice:

= Selection(2,"red","blue","green) "/ returns" blue

Translate

The Transpose feature helps you to transfer vertical data to horizontal, and vice versa easily.

{= conversion(b4: c9)}

Note: Transpose is a formula and is dynamic as such. If you only need to do a single transposition process, use the special paste instead.

Offsetting

The offset function is useful for complex ranges of any kind. It allows you to define the row and column offsets from the starting position, and also the final row and column size. The effect is a selection that can dynamically respond to changing conditions and inputs. You can feed this range into other functions, such as the screen below, where offset generates a range that is supplied with the sum function:

= sum(offset(b4,1,i4,4,1)))) / q3 sum;

Continuous

The indirect feature lets you create references as text. At first, this definition is a little difficult to grasp, but in certain cases, it can be useful. Below, we use the indirect to obtain cell a1 values in 5 separate worksheets. Every single reference is dynamic. If the name of the sheet changes, then update the guide.

= **Indirect**(b5&"!a1) "/ = Blank! a1

The indirect function is likewise used to "lock" references so that they will not change when adding or deleting rows or columns. See related examples at the bottom of the Indirect Feature page for more information.

Caution: all offset and indirect functions are unpredictable, and can slow down large or complicated spreadsheets.

Statistical Features

Say and count

You can count count numbers using count function, and count non-empty cells. You could count blank cells with countblank, but we count blank cells with counter in the screen below, which is usually more useful.

= count(b5: f5) / Numbers count

= counta(b5: f5) / The number and text numbers

= countif(b5: f5,") "/ Blank count

Councils and councillors

For conditional counts, one criterion can be added to the countif function. Various criteria may be implemented simultaneously in council function:

= Cuntif(c5: c12,"red) "/ Red count

= countif(f5: f12,">50) "/ total value > 50

= c5: c12,"red",d5: d12,"tx) "/ red and tx

= countives(c5: c12,"blue,"f5: f12,">50)

Summe, list, list

To sum up, using the feature Description. Using sumifs or sumifs, to sum up conditionally. Following this same pattern as the counting functions, the function sumif can only apply one criterion while the function sumifs can apply multiple criteria.

= sum(f5: f12), / All

= sumif(c5: c12,"red,"f5: f12) / just red

= sumif(f5: f12,">50) "/ greater than 50

= sumifs(f5: f12,c5: c12,"red,"d5: d12,")

= sumifs(f5: f12,c5: c12,"blu,"f5: f12,">50)

The one, one and average

Following the same method, you can measure the mean, average, and average.

= Average(f5: f12)/ All

= Averageif(c5: c12,"red,"f5: f12)/ just red

= f5: f12,c5: c12,"red",d5: d12,"tx) "/ red and tx

Min, Max, Big, Little

The largest and smallest values can be identified with max and min, and the nth largest and smallest with large and low. "Info" in the screen below is the range called c5:c13, used in all formulas.

= max(data) / ...

= min(data) / Minimum

= Large(data,1) / Maximum 1st

= width(data,2) / 2nd biggest

= Large(data,3)/ Largest 3rd

= Small(data,1) / 1st Lesser

= Small(data,2) / Minimum 2nd

= Small(data,3) / Less 3rd

Small ones, maxifs

The minivans and the maxives. Such functions help you to find minimum and maximum conditions values:

= maxifs(d5: d15,c5: c15,"female) "/

= maxifs(d5: d15,c5: c15,"male) "/ Male Top

= minifs(d5: d15,c5: c15,"female) "/ Lowest Women

= minifs(d5: d15,c5: c15,"male) "/ Male Lowest

Note: new minifs and maxifs are available in excel through office 365 and excellent 2019.

Wear style

The mode function returns the number most frequently occurring within the range:

Returns 1 = mode(b5: g5)/

Rating

Using the rank function to order values from smallest to smallest, or from smallest to largest:

Mathematical Functions

ABST

The abs function is used to convert negative values to positive.

Returns = abs(-134.50)/ 134.50

Rand and edge between

Both the function rand and the function randbewteen will produce random numbers on the fly. Rand produces long decimal numbers from zero to 1 Randbetween produces random integer numbers between two given numbers.

= rand) (/ of zero to 1

= 1 to 100 randbetween(1,100)/

Round, rounddown, int

Using the Round feature to round up or down values. Use roundup to force rounding down to a given number of digits. Using rounddown to force a rounddown. Using the int function to dispose of the decimal part of a number altogether.

= Round(11.777,1)/ 11.8 returns

Returns 11.8 = roundup(11.777)/

= 11.777,1) / returns 11.7

Returns 11 = int(11.777)/

Mround, board, ceiling

Using mround feature to round values to the nearest number. Role of the floor and ceiling often round to a given multiple. Rounding down floor forces, and rounding up ceiling forces.

= back(13.85,.25)/ returns 13.75

= Overhead(13.85,.25)/ returns 14

Returns 13.75 = floor(13.85,.25)/

Modification

After division, the mod feature returns the remaining. This sounds boring and geeky, but mod appears in all kinds of formulas, particularly formulas that have something to do "every nth time."

Description

The sumproduct feature is a strong and flexible tool when managing data of all types. You can easily use sumproducts to count and sum based on parameters, and you can use them in elegant ways that simply don't work with countives and sumifs. We use sumproducts in the screen below for counting and summing orders in march. For information and links to several examples, see the Overview tab.

= Sumproduct(—(month(b5: b12)=3))) / March count

= Summaries(—(month(b5: b12)=3),c5: c12) / Summaries

Subtle

The subtotal function is an 'aggregate function' capable of performing a variety of operations on a data set. All told, subtotal can do 11 operations, including number, average, count, max, min, etc. (see the full list on this page). The key feature of the subtotal is that it excludes rows that were "filtered out" from the Excel table and, optionally, rows that were covered manually. In the screen below, only the seven visible rows in the table are counted and summed by subtotal:

Returns 7 = subtotal(3,b5: b14)/

= 9.54 returns subtotal(9,f5: f14)/

Collect

The aggregate method, like subtotal, can also run several aggregate operations on a collection of data and can optionally ignore hidden rows. The main differences are that aggregate can run more operations (total 19) and can disregard errors too.

Aggregate is used in the screen below to perform min, max, large and small operations while ignoring any errors. An error in cell b9 will normally prevent those functions from returning the result.

Look at this page for a comprehensive list of operations that can be performed by aggregate.

= aggregate(4,6,values) / Ignoring errors max, returning 100

= aggregate(5,6,values) / min miss errors, returns 75

Role Text

Left, right, halfway level

Using the functions left, right, and mid to remove characters from the left, right, or middle of the text:

= left('abc-1234-red',3)/ returns 'abc'

= mid("abc-1234-red,"5,4) / "1234" returns

= right('abc-1234-red',3) / returns rot.

Len

This function returns the length of a string. Len occurs in many formulae counting words or characters.

Scan, find

Use the find function or search function to search for specific text within a cell. These functions return the corresponding text numerical location, but search makes wildcards, and finding is case-sensitive. Where text is not found, both functions will throw an error, so wrap the isnumber function to return true or false.

Replace

Use the Replace feature to replace text by location. Use the Substitution feature to replace text by matching. Remove the two asterisks (**) in the first example by replacing the first two characters with an empty string ('."). In the second case, all hash characters (#) are deleted by replacing "#" with "»."

= Substitute ("**red,"1, 2,") "/ returns "red"

= replacement ("##red #," "#,") ""/ returns" gold

Code

Use the code feature to find out the numeric code for a character. Using the char feature to retranslate numeric code to a character. In the example below, each character in column b is translated by code to its corresponding code. The char converts the code back to a character in column f.

=('a') / returns 97

Returns "a" = char(97)/

Trim, tidy

Use the trim feature to dispose of extra space in the text. Using clean for eliminating line breaks and other non-printing characters.

= trim(a1) / Extra room delete

= Clean(a1) / Stretch line breaks

Concat, wordpiece, concatenate

Concat and Textjoin are new in Excel through office 365. The concat function allows you to concatenate (join) several values, including a set of non-delimiting values. The textjoin feature does the same but allows you to define a delimiter and can ignore empty values as well.

= textjoin(",",true, b4: h4) / returns "red , white, green, pink, black"

= concat(b7: h7)/ "8675309" returns

Excel also offers a concatenate function, but there are no special features to it. I wouldn't bother with it and would concatenate with the ampersand (&) character in a formula instead.

Exactly

The exact feature lets you compare two strings of text in a case-sensitive manner.

Upper, middle, right

Use the upper, lower and proper feature to alter the text case

= Brown Sue) (/ returns "Pink Sue"

= Lower("Blue Sue")/ returns "Gray Sue"

= proper("Brown Sue) "/ returns" Brown Sue

Last but not least, the text feature is certainly one. The text feature enables the number formatting to be applied as text to numbers (including dates, times, etc.) It's especially useful if you need to include a specified number in a message such as "sale ends on [date]."

= letter(b5,"$#,#0.00)

= (b6,"000000)

= "save" & text(b7,"0%")

= "end of sale"&text(b8,"mmm d")

WHAT IS VBA?

VBA stands for Visual Basic for Applications. Excel VBA is the programming language of Microsoft for Excel and all other Microsoft Office applications, such as word and PowerPoint. They all share a common programming language in the office suite programs.

Why use Vba Excel?

While users can not control the main excel program directly via VBA, they can still master the art of creating macros to maximize their time in excel. There are two methods of doing macros excel.

First, the use of a macro recorder. Excel would record all steps a user makes after triggering the file and save it as a "flow," known as a macro. This macro is saved when the user finishes the recorder and can be allocated to a button that will run the same procedure again when pressed. This method is fairly simple and does not require inherent VBA code knowledge. The method is going to work for simple processes.

The disadvantage of this approach, however, is that it is not very flexible, and the macro will exactly imitate the user's input. Recorder macros often use absolute referencing by default instead of conditional referencing. Ikt means macros made in this way are incredibly difficult to use with variables and "smart" processes.

The second and more efficient way to build an Excel macro is by coding one using VBA.

Where to code excel VBA?

Press alt + f11 inside any Office software to access the VBA pane. This will open a window with a file structure tree at the top left, properties at the bottom left, a debug pane at the bottom center and the bottom right, and a coding section that encompasses most of the screen at the center and top right. At first, this may sound daunting, but in fact, it's simpler than it seems.

The consumer will, most of the time, function in the Coding area. The segment File Structure is only used to create a new macro script. The more advanced macros that use user forms to build graphical interfaces for the macro can use the Property section in the bottom left.

The coding section is where coding happens the most, if not all. The user can build and code macros and save them here. After the macro code has been written and saved, other triggers in the Excel model can then be added. The macro can be triggered by pressing a specific button on the worksheet, or by changing certain cells, for example. To execute a macro, the simplest way is to add it to a button.

What is VBA, then?

The acronym VBA stands for the Visual Basic Applications. This is an offshoot of the basic visual programming language that Microsoft developed back in the 1990s, allowing Microsoft programs to interact with each other based on events or activities taking place within those programs. This language is used not only in workplace programs such as Excel and PowerPoint but also in applications such as notepad and painting. Since Microsoft developed this language to complement its own applications, the code is very intuitive to the user. For example, if you read in Excel a code line stating range('a1: b4').clearcontents, you can make a well-educated guess that the code line tells Excel to clear the contents of cells a1 through b4. This is enormous as it helps people with very little or no experience of computer programming to pick up on how the VBA language functions quickly.

What are those macros?

Macros are the ones most people use while writing VBA code. A macro (also called a process or a subroutine) is a grouping of code executing a set of tasks or commands within a specific computer program (aka application). The macros will contain code performing calculations, copying & pasting, formatting changes, and a lot of other nifty things, all in milliseconds! Most office users use macros to automate repetitive activities that take them a long time (by the keyboard & mouse) to execute manually.

What is the "Low" function?

I threw this section in particular for a friend of mine who was frustrated by the lack of introductory VBA content. He said, "Chris, I've been looking everywhere, and I wish there was a simple introduction to VBA that could get me started. I mean, I can't even figure out what a dim heck is!" so below, I'll list a few words you might have come across if you've ever reported a macro of VBA code you've seen. If there are any other terms you have come across and would like to be described, leave a comment below.

Dim- this means dimension and is a declaration used to announce the name and form of the variable you want to construct.

Sub- this is a short subroutine comment, and your code opening phrase. A new macro or process is generated each time sub is typed. To inform VBA that your process is over, the words "end sub" must be put as the last line of code for your macro.

Module- this is the field where you can write your macro codes and functions. This is also the place where you store any macros you have.

Class module- this is a truly specialized environment for VBA users. You can write your own personalized classes, methods, and collections into the VBA library in this area. I 'd stay away for learning if you're a novice. This form of functionality will never be used by most VBA writers throughout their careers, but it's a very powerful choice if needed.

Feature- VBA lets you build your own custom functions. This can be either used by your macros to achieve a certain output or used in the Excel formula bar to measure the values of your cell.

Userforms- these are pop-up boxes that allow users to enter inputs or select options. Microsoft uses these in its software all the time. Examples include error message frames, dialogue boxes, and macro-recorder. The best thing is that VBA allows you to build your own custom user-forms!

You're probably aware that there are thousands of different tasks people use to succeed. Here are only a few examples:

Holding lists of items like client names, student grades, or suggestions for holiday gifts

Budgeting and Forecast

Analyzing science evidence

Invoices and other forms

Developing databank charts

The listings may go on and on, but you get the idea. Excel is used for a wide range of things, and everyone who reads this article has different needs and opinions about Excel. One thing that's popular with virtually every reader is the need to automate any part of excel. That's exactly what VBA is all about.

For example, you could create a VBA program to format your month-end sales report and print it out. You could execute the macro with a single command after creating and checking the program, which will enable excel to perform certain time-consuming procedures automatically. Instead of battling through a boring sequence of commands, you should grab a cup of joe and let your machine do the job — what's it supposed to be like, right?

These are a few brief explanations of some common VBA macros usages. You can push one or two of them over your screen.

Attach a list of texts

If you want to enter your company name frequently in the worksheets, you can create a macro for you to type in. You can expand the definition to any degree you want. You might, for example, create a macro that automatically types a list of all the salespeople working for your company.

Automation of a task you frequently do

Suppose you're a sales manager and you need a month-end sales report to keep your boss satisfied. If the job is straightforward, a VBA program can be built to do that for you. The consistently high quality of your reports will impress your manager, and you will be promoted to a new job for which you are extremely unqualified.

Automatisation of repeated operations

You can record a macro while performing the task on the first workbook and then let the macro replicate your action on the other workbooks if you need to perform the same action on, say, 12 separate excel workbooks. The good thing about this is that Excel never laments being bored. Excel 's macro recorder is similar to the sound recorded on a tape recorder. But they don't need a microphone.

Creation of a custom order

Do you mostly issue the same sequence of commands to the Excel menu? If so, save a few seconds by developing a macro that combines these commands into a single custom command that can be executed with a single keystroke or button press.

Build your own custom toolbar button

You can use your own buttons to customize the Excel toolbars which run the macros you write. This sort of thing appears to make office staff very impressed.

Create a custom control menu

You can also customize the excel menus with your own commands that run the macros you're writing to. That impresses office workers even more.

Simplified front finishing

You can find plenty of people in almost every workplace who don't even understand how to use computers. Use vba (sound familiar?); you can make it easy for those novice users to do some useful work. You could set up a foolproof data-entry template, for example, so you don't have to waste your time doing boring work.

Create new features for worksheet

Although excel contains a variety of built-in functions (such as sum and average), you can build custom worksheet functions that can simplify your formulas considerably. You are going to be surprised by how simple it is. Even yet, the insert feature dialogue box shows your custom functions, making them appear to be built-in—very frivolous stuff.

Creation of full, macro-driven applications

You can use vba to build large-scale applications with custom dialogue boxes, on-screen support, and lots of other accouterments if you're willing to invest some time.

Build custom Excel add-ins

You're already familiar with some of the complements that Excel ships with. Analysis toolpak, for example, is a common add-in. You can build your own special purpose add-ins using vba.

How to use Excel vba Editor

Excel's Visual Basic (vba) editor is a very effective tool for applications.

It allows you to write and edit custom scripts that automate Excel actions.

In reality, it is stored in vba code in the vba editor when you record a macro.

But writing a macro directly from the vba editor gives you more versatility than the conventional way of recording a macro.

By working directly with the visual basic for applications, you can build better code and complete more complicated tasks.

In this tutorial, I'll teach you the basics of how to use vba editor for excel. Let's get home!

* This guide is for windows to excel in 2019. Did they have a different version? No issue, you still have the exact same steps to take.

Come on now

What's the Editor of vba?

The Program Editor Visual Basic, also called the vba editor, vb editor, or vbe is a script development interface.

Vba is the programming language used by such scripts.

Visual basic is a complete programming language, but you'll just need to know some of the basics to get vba scripts hanging in excel.

If you did some (ide) programming in an integrated development environment, the vba editor looks familiar. It lets you build, manage and run your Excel spreadsheet with vba code.

Let's look at the way it's opened and do some simple stuff.

When to use the editor on vba

You'll need to open the vba editor before you start encoding. To do this, move to the Developer tab and click on the Simple Visual button:

If you do not see the Developer button, go to File > Options > Customize the Ribbon and search the "Developer" button in the right pane.

You can also open the vba editor using the Alt + f11 keyboard shortcut.

The vba editor is, as you can see, packed full of buttons, menus and options. Don't worry – in this route, we'll go through the relevant ones.

We will concentrate on the most basic sections of vba editor in this guide.

In the left-hand window, the project view has a tab called modules.

This folder includes vba modules, which are like application containers. These are included in the module when capturing macros.

If you want to write your own code, the code will be stored in a module.

Click on VBA project (book1) to attach a new, empty module and go to Insert > Modul.

If no modules folder existed in the VBA project, the folder would be generated, and a new module will be within. This is where your vba code will be put when you're ready to write it.

To uninstall a module, right-click it in the left pane and choose Select [name of the module].

Excel will suggest that you confirm the withdrawal. If you want to save the part, you can export it.

Finally, let's look at executing a vba editor macro.

You can execute it from this view after you have built a macro, either by coding it directly or by recording it from the standard excel interface.

Only press the Macro button in the menu bar to run a macro:

You can click f5 on the keyboard, too.

Then move on to vba

This was a very important introduction to the vba editor.

You'll see as you write more vba code that the vba editor is better support for you in your work.

For the time being, play around with the editor and get a feel for where the buttons and menus are, and get used to the vba layout.

HOW TO USE THE VBA FOR DATA AUTOMATION IN EXCEL, CREATING VBA IN EXCEL TO AUTOMATE VARIOUS TASKS

Application Visual Basic (vba) can be used to automate nearly all of the goods in every Microsoft office (ms office). If you have a simple understanding of vba but no specific application for its use yet, this article will give you just that: real-life, functional examples of full vba procedures that transform entire business processes into a click of a button.I'm going to take you through the development of a composite key and find all the records from a server that fit those in our master list. Then we're going to examine the non-matching records using some pivot tables to aid pattern recognition.

Far more important is to learn the right attitude to make vba work for you than to learn the code. Vba will save you time and make you a rockstar at work, but you need to use it wisely as with any great strength. We will address the basic change in attitude that occurs when you start working with vba, and how you and your business can make that attitude work.

"The Macro Approach"

When you've successfully automated everything relevant to your job at vba, you've probably adopted a whole new outlook on ms office products (no pun intended), particularly excellent. This new mentality benefits from an appreciation of the object hierarchy of these applications, or even from the successful use of the macro recorder.

You start searching for more macro projects that could potentially save you a lot of time once you understand how macros work. So long a macro is defined as a way of mapping input parameters to output parameters, often to automate work, then describing your mindset shift from a fundamentally "manual mindset" to a "macro mindset" should be appropriate.

This latest macro mentality will trigger problems if you don't use it when it comes to how organizations operate. Yeah, it'd be good if you were able to automate any job that touches excel, but what is the cost of the opportunity?

Two questions you should bear in mind are: "how long does it take?" and "is there similar functionality in another program that we have or will have in the near future?"

Let's look at how to learn the right way to go while using vba.

Comprehend the meaning of your automation project

The first thing you need to do, as with any project, is considered the meaning of the process you want to automate. Create a timeline to help explain projections of the deadlines and life expectancy for each solution.

Be sure that you understand the drawbacks of using the vba process as a solution and any alternatives. For instance, if your department invests in a new business intelligence tool that can solve the problem, you should investigate that tool before you write any vba code.

Track the timeline.

Know how long it will take you to finish writing your vba script, how long it should take you to execute the task manually, and how long it should take. Will the business process change drastically in a few months, and does it break your code?

Decisions about procurement and allocation of resources may reduce the life expectancy of your application. So, see that there is a possibility of spending your time creating a vba solution that will either be replaced in a few weeks by a business intelligence tool or made redundant due to an unexpected shift in the business process (e.g., the business process was unique to the company you worked with, and they terminated their agreement with your business).

As business intelligence tool licenses could cost thousands of dollars and most businesses use ms office by default, I think the probability of starting a vba project is much smaller, finding it no longer viable, and then abandoning it altogether. Instead, you might explore the features of a new business intelligence tool, spend hours educating yourself on how to use it, and then find out that compatibility problems (or other unexpected limitations) with it occur.

One last word about context: if you're trying to find the best opportunities to use vba, you'll find it in small companies, downsizing companies, or even large corporate divisions that operate on a low budget. In general, businesses and agencies that seek to save money should be even more open to using vba as a solution.

Keep those general rules in mind when choosing the vba path:

1) Great vba strategies when money-saving is a high priority.

2) Highly versatile approaches, vba.

3) The vba solutions are better supported and used for the least number of users possible.

4) The vba solutions are in the vast majority in Excel.

5) Smaller companies usually have greater chances of vba than bigger firms.

6) Vba solutions are as robust as you are in the process of making them.

The main point of macros and vba is to save time (and yes, add features, but our emphasis here is time), and as long as you're saving time, then the macro mentality will work for you rather than against you.

Let's just look at the real code now.

Test 1: lookup method for software code

For those of you who are relatively new to vba, a sequence of vba statements is an individually functional method.

The basic concept for this sampling method is to determine whether or not goods in the product report file contain new product specification codes for the item catalog category (i.e., product specifications that do not currently exist in the master file) and, if so, which line items do they contain and how many?

I use a text file, product report to represent a third-party report for this example. The baseline file is an excellent workbook that stores historical product data.

I recommend you first search the "prodcodelookup2" code for the GitHub in its entirety. I'll break it down in the parts below.

Broken down prodcodelookup2

Perhaps the most critical part of problem-solving is the ability to break them down into pieces and methodically approach them. The most logical solution for me is to write every block of code based on the order in which a user would execute the function if it were performed manually.

I subsequently refine my method based on a more nuanced understanding of the object model and rewrite it using far less code. (For purposes of consistency and readability, you may want to change the order in which these tasks should be performed. Hold this thought going, as we will come back to it later.)

Here's the first useful piece of code here:

Notice that the method name fits the Pascal case and ends with the version number, which is helpful when you find alternate ways to write code. It's extremely painful to remember that you forgot to move to a revision while you're troubleshooting, and the mistake you made broke your original, previously working code! So always refresh your processes, keep working copies.

The very 1st statement (line 5) that I (and most people write on stack overflow) is solely for performance benefit. Screenupdating is an application object property that regulates whether your screen updates the behavior your macro does in real-time or not. By switching off the screenupdate property, you won't see the magic until your code finishes running, but you'll find much faster running times when you get into loops. While I have not reset the property to real, it is probably a good idea to do so at the very end of your code (unless you have a reason not to).

Witness now to my extraordinary imagination and humor, as shown in the following variable names:

All right, the names may not be witty or creative, but when you start debugging code, you don't want to be witty and creative. Easy and concise variable names are what will save the day when anything falls.

I found it easier to control variables by grouping them by type and feature of data (meaning how I use them). For example, all range variables beginning with rng are important for controlling how and when I find which columns and table parts I want to work with.

It's also worth noting that my lookup variables are all defined close to each other. If you start writing longer procedures, inserting comments, and reserving a new line and "small" keyword for each may be helpful.

Making a habit out of such activity can make it simpler for you while your code is being troubleshot or revised. For example, the same block in the style I have defined is rewritten here:

You get the idea; just type the name of the variable into words or short phrases that explain how you use it. This part is relatively easy to understand but highly significant.

Assign object variables to workbook names and worksheets. This behavior has many benefits, including efficiency and readability. As you get more familiar with vba, you may opt-out of this practice — the primary aim is to make it as easy as possible to troubleshoot and maintain your code. If you and potential users are not taking advantage of this activity, then feel free to omit it.

Assign objects like this to your workbook and worksheet variables (yes, order matters — workbooks first, since they are parent objects):

Since I can't top off his beautifully succinct definition, here's a link to John Walkenbach 's website and a brief summary that tells you everything you need to know about object variables.

Let's go over the next section:

Start time is a non-constant which holds the initial value of the timer property and is used to measure the cumulative runtime at the end. If you wish, you may build short variables for longer string values, which you can need to reference many times. Exemplify this definition by the variables "icc" and "pc."

Finally, the last line in this section specifies the framework for the lines of code that follow. (Sure, you don't want the compiler to guess which workbook or worksheet to use, so be sure to specify it.)

A few planning and formatting operations are in order until generating the "prodcombo" composite key (lines 31–42). Hide columns that are unrelated to this phase in the baseline workbook, create new columns that we care about, and add bold formatting for readability on all headers.

On lines 44 to 52, turn on filtering for all headers and then filter out all but labels (let's say we're only interested in this product specification).

In lines 53 through 69, I use a loop to construct a prodcombo, concatenate values in five columns, and use a space boundary.

It is necessary to remove blank products which are intended for lines 70 through 78. For this example, because we are concerned only with products which have values in at least one of the five fields, we do not need records which are blank in all five fields.

Notice the statement on line 80 referring to another procedure: "now run prodcodelookup2"

I originally wrote and checked two different procedures: one for formatting and other accompanying functions, and the other for vlookup execution. I don't generally recommend doing the same thing, but because it was my first time using a loop vlookup, I found it easier to learn that way. The prodcodelookup2 procedure executes a vlookup on each cell under the specified header and loops through all records until the end of the table is reached.

Let's talk about a few tips to tackle vlookups in vba before we look at the second example.

Tips on using vlookups in vba

Blanks and errors (basically anything that returns the default error status from a manually executed vlookup function) would cause the whole system to crash. Yeah, that is true. This method requires you to incorporate error handling in your code while operating with vlookup in vba.

There's at least one useful example for vlookups explicitly on stack overflow on error handling. Wrap the loop with the function in lines 83 and 96, as I did in the illustration, and this will easily solve the problem.

Then perform the following tasks over the last few lines (98–109):

1) identify the location of the prodcode column header by column name.

2) use the "count" function of the worksheet on all values under prodcode and assign them to a variable.

3) Return the result into a message box to the recipient.

4) Switchback on screenupdating.

5) Return in seconds, the time it took for the application to run.

6) View the user 's time in a message box.

That concludes the script for the first Vba. So, right now, you still think, "Oh! where's the data analysis?"

Test data: sample 2

All right, so this information is useful, but what about the other products? How do these findings compare to the other groups of requirements (besides labels), and what forms of comparisons are worthy of our attention? How about all the non-matching goods, and what should we know about them?

To make it a bit more complicated, let's add a status flag to the goods. The status reflects whether the product specification code at issue is active or not.

For a fast recap, the dimensions of our study can be accurately summarized for 'product type,' 'active/inactive status,' and 'play/no play status.' With this additional information, we have several use cases for pivot table data visualization.

Where's the data analysis? Right here, in a distinct procedure:

It is a longer method, using pivot tables. Those two features by themselves explain a shortlist of tips to bear in mind when writing your own version:

1) Avoid ".select": often, for performance purposes, seek to avoid using the process ".select" or the object ".select." Try to look up the methods and resources you're using and think about ways to avoid selecting them.

2) Recording macros experiment: the macro recording function helps you to quickly learn some of the important bits of syntax in addition to widely used methods, objects, and properties.

3) Write comments: taking the time to assign meaningful names to the variables and regularly use

white space are surprisingly useful ways of making the code more readable. As you write lengthy and increasingly complex procedures, the associated advantages will become evident.

4) Performance: I'll mention just a few simple but very effective performance tricks that will make a big difference as you move forward. The vb editor uses something called "dot processing," which simply means interpreting the vba code by the time intervals (dots). In that, the number of lines, the number of statements that need to be compiled, is reduced. Finally, this approach will benefit you considerably more as the procedures grow in size and complexity.

5) Learn how to reference r1c1 cells: since the macro recorder uses it, you should know how to read it and familiarize yourself with this reference style — especially to learn how pivot tables work in vba.

Remember the thought I told you to hold on (i.e., change the order in which you schedule tasks from the order in which they are performed manually)? Now is the time to revisit the notion.

As I wrote the "prodflag v3" method, I found it difficult to copy, paste, and remove operations. I didn't really understand how the.cutcopymode property works, and I had to get the code to work – and fast.

Luckily, in the end, I learned a valuable lesson:

The order in which activities are carried out manually does not necessarily correlate to the order in which they should be carried out in vba.

Although there are benefits to knowing how a function is done manually, the main concern is not to enable your thought to be limited – such limitations can result in inefficient code that includes needless commands.

In this example (lines 1–36), we copy blank (alternatively, 'nospec' or 'spec-less') records into a new analytical workbook. Originally, I figured it would be easier to copy everything from the paper to the review sheet and filter it out later. As I've learned the hard way, filtering first can be faster.

You'll want to pay attention to lines 18, 20, and 21 after you write a code summary and define the variables. Think of the prtable object variable as a reference identified on a specified worksheet by the upper-left and bottom-right corners of a given range.

I intentionally chose cell "a1" because I knew that all the most relevant report data began in the first column. I'm going to discuss one way of later having the dynamic.

Lines 20 and 21 reflect a syntax for new worksheet development. Since I'm storing this macro with the results of the analysis in the same workbook, I'm only making sure it's "oriented" (i.e., "active") before running the macro.

Lines 23 through 25 declare the object variable of the previously generated worksheet, assign a value to the variable "finalrow" and add auto filters to the worksheet for export. The following block (lines 27–30) consists of a "for-each" loop that filters out all, except blanks, for the spec data column records.

Copying and pasting between workbooks is the task of a code block consisting of lines 32 through 36. Notice how I described the set of data that I would like to copy (without using.select): line 32 contains a very useful ".resize" method with two arguments, the prtablerows variable and the number seven, representing the number of rows and columns that I want to copy.

If you were curious, line 38 is not an error; here, I intentionally reassigned the final line value because it had to be reset. Know how this was included in row 28? By the end of the "for-each" loop, its value is equal to the table's number of columns, which is not the value we want it to use for this next loop. You can get some pretty weird results if you don't reset it in loops!

For aesthetic (and practical) purposes, I added lines 39 to 50 to construct a for-each loop with a statement nesting inside it. The code effectively adjusts the values color and font depending on whether the records are marked as active or inactive. I need to explain one important detail at this stage to prevent misunderstanding.

The active/inactive status flag is not programmed in the code; it is written in the database. You may equate the logic associated with my active/inactive flag, and imitate it for your own purposes if you construct your own flag.

On line 52, I switched on the auto filter key, then dynamically searched for my first header of interest (the item status column, i.e., the status flag), and assigned it to an object variable.

Lines 53 to 55 help us scan all the cells within a range and find one cell based on its text value:

There are two crucial aspects of the statement I want you to focus on saving time:

1) The "lookat" argument in the ".find" method has two constants: "xlpart" and "xlwhole." If you use "xlpart," then the method will scan all the cells inside the range and stop at the first one containing the string you are using. You may not want to use "xlpart" if there is a risk that you may have a header repeatedly

containing the same word, because if the command changes, it can pick the wrong header. I highly suggest sticking to "xlwhole" for this purpose.

2) define the set by the name of the worksheet. Also, the activesheet is better than no qualification; it is a guide to best practices, which will make your life simpler.

Vlookups aren't the only important worksheet to use in vba. I used the "countif" function in lines 57 and 58 to search all the values in our item status column and assign the results to the corresponding active and inactive variables. If you skip to the message box on lines 204 to 206, I will use these variables to return the results to the user.

Rather than going through each of the pivot tables one by one, I'll save a lot of time for both of us by summarizing the method and describing the pivot tables programming trick to you.

For vba, using the pivot tables.

In vba, the preconditions for pivoting tables are the same, conceptually, as they are for a user who creates them manually: verify that your data source contains true, structured, high-quality data. The same holds true in my particular example (sample 2): build the test data for an imaginary product, its categories, and its specifications.

Are you ready to learn this magic? You're about to find out how one of the most commonly used, advanced features of Excel can be automated. All right, here we go:

1) Copy those two lines I used (lines 63 and 64).

2) Navigate to your workbook, click on the Developer tab, and then press "Macro log."

3) left-click a cell in the pivot data table you want to use, and press "ctrl" + "a" to pick all the cells.

4) Press "alt" + "n" + "v" + "enter" (or click "open" to change any settings).

5) Manually build your pivot table by dragging the correct dimensions of the columns you like, filtering, grouping, formatting the values, etc.

6) Click again on "Macro log" button.

7) Click on "alt" and "f11" to return to the vb editor window and find the code in the module in which you logged it.

8) Print it, paste it under the worksheet you built into your project, and read it out.

9) Repeat as many pivoting tables and worksheets as your heart can wish.

Are you soothed? The idea here is that you do not have to worry too much about the pivot table objects and methods; automating pivot tables is most effective when you do it manually with the recorder once, and then reading the code a few times if you are interested in moving variables or changing constants.

Compare this method with the v-lookup programming process, which involves error handling, a clearly defined table or range allocated to an object variable (and qualified by an object worksheet), and contained within a loop. There's nothing macro-recorder friendly about that!

If you plan to use more macro recorder (even if it's just for pivot tables), I've got one more suggestion.

Do a favor to yourself: know the style r1c1

It's certainly not the cell-referencing type you're used to, but the macro-recorder uses r1c1. I recommend familiarizing yourself with it to save time when working with pivot tables, in particular, so you have less work to do when editing the macro recorder produced code.

It is up to you from here on to find out which pivot table artifacts are worth learning in vba. The truth is that, once you understand some keyboard shortcuts, how to set up your tables properly and how to prepare your code to insert blocks of registered pivot tables, you can automate a workbook that contains 20 pivot tables in a matter of minutes.

Allocate your time effectively

The two most critical components of automated analysis (in terms of the most effective way possible) are as follows:

1) Maximum effort should be made to prepare the data. Make sure the consistency of the data is top-notch, and think about any flags, keys, authentication, reconciliation, and basic calculations you may like.

2) Visualize the end result as you build and refine your chart.

I bet you are, at this stage, shocked. You probably did not expect this article to concentrate so little on the actual vba code involved in the creation of pivot tables, charts, and other objects and properties that could be used to analyze the data.

You don't save much of your time learning all the code needed to create a pivot table — that's a surprisingly time-consuming job. Alternatively, learn how to plan the collection of data and automate the preparation itself.

Using vba can similarly save you time and energy, but using it effectively and wisely will benefit you most.

DOS AND DON'TS OF INSERTING DATA IN EXCEL.

Inputting data correctly into a spreadsheet first prevents issues later and makes it easier to use all of the excel resources and features like formulas and maps. This guide covers basic doses and data entries in spreadsheet programs such as excel, google papers, and calc open office.

Instructions for Excel 2019, 2016, 2013, 2010; Excel for Mac, Excel for Office 365, and Excel online.

Overview of excel data entry

Excel worksheets are strong analytics tools that store data in large quantities. Make sure the data is correctly presented and evaluated using the best data entry practices in excel.

These are the main dos and shouldn't bear in mind when using excel:

Plan the scoreboard.

Do not leave rows or columns vacant when entering related data.

Do save sometimes and save in two places.

Do not use numbers as headings for columns, and do not include data units.

In formulas, using cell comparisons and celled ranges.

Do not leave cells unlocked, which contain formulas.

Filter the data yourself.

Project the scoreboard

It is a good idea to prepare before you start typing while entering the data into Excel. Decide how to use the worksheet, the data found therein and what to do with that data. The final layout of the worksheet is greatly influenced by those decisions.

If the spreadsheet needs to be reorganized to make it more effective, preparing before typing saves time later.

When preparing your excellent workbooks, here are a few things to consider:

What is the function of the Table?

How much data does the spreadsheet hold?

Need the charts?

Were the spreadsheets printed?

What is the function of the Table?

The spreadsheet purpose defines the location of the data because the most sensitive information needs to be visible and easily available. Where calculations are needed for your data, calculations shall decide which formulas and functions are needed and where the formulas should be entered.

How much data does the spreadsheet hold?

Initially, the amount of data the spreadsheet contains and how much is applied to it later dictates the number of worksheets you will need for the workbook.

Here are only a few suggestions:

Don't over-spread your info. Clear information can be difficult to locate when the data are found in many worksheets. Calculations that span multiple worksheets or workbooks often affect the output of excel.

For large worksheets, show substantial column numbers above the column headings, instead of simply finding summary information at the bottom of the worksheet.

Want any charts?

If all or part of the data is used in a map or charts, the information structure may be affected.

When using maps, follow these best practices:

Data can need to be grouped differently according to the form of a map. Create a description region, for example, for the pie charts.

For large spreadsheets, transfer the charts to separate pages to avoid crowding worksheets with data and images.

Were the spreadsheets printed?

How the data is stored depends on how the data is written. Should any or only any of the data be printed? Is the data going to be displayed in portrait or landscape layout?

Hold those tips in mind when printing worksheets:

If the worksheet is printed using a portrait view on letter size paper (8.5 " x 11), "put the majority of the data under a few columns in the rows. Thus headings can be seen on one board.

Display column headings at the top of each page, if the worksheet is written on several sheets. Column headings provide a summary of the data and make the data easier to read and more accessible.

When printing multiple columns of details, use the landscape style to keep all headings on one tab. Again, print the column headings at the top of each page, if multiple sheets are needed.

If the worksheet includes charts, transfer the charts before printing the workbook to a separate page.

Do not leave the rows or columns blank when entering related data.

Blank rows or columns in data tables or similar data ranges, make it difficult to properly use certain features of Excel, such as maps, pivot tables, and unique functions.

Also, blank cells containing data in a row or column may cause problems, as seen in the image below.

The absence of empty spaces helps to excel in the identification and collection of relevant data while using a variety of functions such as sorting, filtering, or autosum.

Using borders or format headings and labels when you want to break up data to make it easier to read. To isolate and highlight the data, use visual signals such as bold text, lines, and cell color.

When working with the data in rows and columns, follow these tips:

Place a descriptive heading at the top of the table's first column, with the data below.

Where there is more than one data set, list them one by one in columns (left to right) with the title at the top of each data series.

Hold separate unrelated data.

Although it is important to keep the related data together, separating different data ranges is also useful. Leave blank columns or rows on the worksheet between different data ranges or other data so that excel selects the right relevant ranges or data tables.

Do save also

Often the value of saving your work can not be overestimated or too frequently mentioned. If you're using a web-based spreadsheet like google sheets or excelling online, saving is not a problem. There's no save choice for those programs. Instead, the autosave feature automatically saves the spreadsheets to your cloud account.

Save your job after two or three modifications to desktop spreadsheet programs. For example, save after adding the data, formatting the column headings, or entering a formula. Save your job every two or three minutes, at least.

While computer and computer device reliability has significantly improved over time, the device still crashes, power failures occur, and other people often leap over your power cord and pull it out of the wall socket. So when incidents happen, data loss raises the workload because you repair what you've already done.

Excel has an autosave feature that typically works really well, but you shouldn't rely on it absolutely. Get used to keeping your data secure with frequent saves.

Shortcuts to Save

You don't need to switch your mouse to a ribbon and select icons to save your work. Instead, get used to saving by using the shortcut keyboard combination. Click ctrl+s, if you want to remove your worksheet.

Save Two Spaces

Store your data in two separate places, as well. The second location is the backup. The safest backup is in a different physical location than the original one.

Consider loading files into your cloud account while loading a backup copy of your workbooks. You would not only have a backup copy in the cloud because workbooks are stored on your computer and in the cloud, but the cloud is configured with redundant backups, which ensure that the data is stored on several servers.

Backups in the Cloud

Once, backups needn't be a time-consuming process.

If protection isn't a concern, such as if your worksheet is a list of your dvd's, it's probably enough to give you a copy. If protection is an issue, then cloud storage is an alternative.

The owners of the software back up their servers in the case of electronic spreadsheets, and that includes all user details. But download a copy of that file to your machine to be free.

Do not use numbers as headings for columns, and do not include data units.

Make it easier to use headings at the top of columns and at the beginning of rows to define your results. Yet don't use numbers like 2012, 2013, etc. as headings.

Column and row headings that are numbers can be unintentionally included in calculations, as seen in the above illustration. When the formulas include functions that automatically pick the data set for the function statement, such as autosum, then the number in the column headings creates a problem.

Usually, these features, which also include automax and autoaverage, will first look for number columns and then search for a number row to the left. The selected set should contain any headings that are numbers.

Numbers used as row headings may be confused as other data series if they are chosen as part of a chart set rather than as axes names.

Format the numbers as text or create text labels in heading cells by preceding each number with an apostrophe (') such as '2012 and '2013. The apostrophe does not appear in the sentence, but the number is added to the text.

Insert units in the titles.

Do not insert currency, temperature, distance, or other units with the number data into each cell. If you do, excel sheets or google sheets would likely display all of your data as text.

Instead, position the units at the top of the column in the headings to ensure that such headings are in text format and do not pose a problem.

Text to the left, digits to the right

If you have text or number data, a fast way to say is to test the alignment of data in the cell. For example, in excel and google sheets, text data is aligned to the left, and the number of data is aligned to the right in the cell.

Although this default alignment is modified, formatting should be implemented after entering all the data and formulas. The default alignment provides you with a hint if the data is correctly formatted in the worksheet.

Currency indications and percent

Inputting data into a worksheet is best achieved by inserting a plain number and then formatting the cell to show the number correctly, for example, as a percentage or as a currency.

Excel and google sheets identify the percentage of symbols that, along with the number, are typed into a cell. These apps often accept common currency symbols, such as the dollar sign ($) or the British pound symbol (£) if you type them into a cell along with the number details, but other currency symbols, such as the South African rand (r), are interpreted as text.

To prevent any future problems, enter the number and then format the currency cell instead of typing the currency symbol.

Using cell references in formulas and designated ranges

Both cell references and named ranges can and should be used to keep formulas and the entire worksheet error-free and up to date.

Cell comparisons are a variation of the letter column and the cell row number such as a1, b23, and w987. Cell references describe the worksheet location of the data.

A specified range or name is similar to a cell reference in that it is used to describe a cell or cell range in a worksheet.

Referencing of formula data

Formulas for conducting calculations such as addition or subtraction are used in excel.

Where the actual number is in formulae such as:

= 5 + 3 Figures

You will need to update the formula each time the data changes. So if the new numbers are 7 and 6 then the formula would be:

= 6 + 7

Instead, if you enter the data into the worksheet cells, use the formula cell references or range names instead of the numbers.

If you enter cell a1 and cell a2 in number 5, then the formula will be:

= 1 + 2

You'll adjust the contents of cells a1 and a2 to update the details, but leave the formula as it is. Excel updates the formula results automatically.

This method is useful when complicated formulas are in the worksheet and when multiple formulas reference the same data. You will then only modify the data at one point, which will then update the formulas that reference it.

Cell references and named ranges often make worksheets safer by shielding the formulas against unintended changes when leaving open data cells.

Tick the details

Another feature of excel and google sheets is that it is possible to insert cell references or range names in formulas using pointing that requires clicking on a cell to insert a reference in the formula. Pointing decreases the probability of errors caused by typing the wrong reference cell or misspelling the name of the unit.

To select data, use the named ranges.

Giving a name to a field of similar data enables the collection of data that will be sorted or filtered.

If the data area size changes, modify the nomenclature set with the name manager.

Do not leave cells unlocked, which contain formulas.

Despite spending too much time getting their formulas correct and using the required cell references, many people make the mistake of leaving those formulas vulnerable to unintentional or unwanted changes.

If you use cell references or named ranges, lock the cells which contain your formulas. Password protects the cells to keep them safe if necessary.

Around the same time, leave the cells that hold the data unlocked so that users can make changes and update the spreadsheet.

Safeguarding a workbook or workbook is a two-step process:

Ensure sure cells are locked correctly.

Secure your worksheet with the addition of a password.

Order the data accordingly

Sort your data after you've finished logging in. Operating with small quantities of unsorted data in excel or google sheets is not normally a concern, but it is challenging to deal with it effectively as the spreadsheet grows bigger.

The data sorted is easier to understand and to evaluate. To return accurate results, certain functions and tools, such as vlookup and subtotal, require sorted data.

Sort the data in various ways, too, to spot patterns that are not obvious at first.

Choose what data to sort.

Excel needs to know the exact set to be sorted and define the relevant data areas if there are:

No blank rows or columns inside the corresponding data field.

Blank rows and columns between corresponding data areas.

Excel also decides if a data area has field names and removes the section from the sorting process.

Allowing excel to select the range for sorting can, however, be risky, particularly with large quantities of data that are difficult to test.

Using names when choosing data

To ensure you select the correct data, highlight the range before starting the type. If you are planning sorting the same data range repeatedly, the best approach is to give it a name.

When sorting a named data set, enter the name in the name box or pick it from the drop-down list associated with it. Excel automatically pinpoints the right data set in the worksheet.

Sorting of cached rows and columns

Excel does not have secret rows and data columns when sorting, so these rows and columns have to be unhidden before sorting occurs. For instance, if row 7 is hidden within a set of data to be sorted, it will remain as row 7 and will not be moved to its correct position in the sorted information.

The same holds true for data columns. Sorting by rows requires reordering data columns, but if column b is secret before sorting, then column b will remain after sorting.

Numbers to store as numbers

Test that all numbers are numbers-formatted. If the outcomes are not what you were expecting, the column that contains numbers that are stored as text and not numbers, for example, negative numbers imported from some accounting systems or a leading apostrophe number ('), are stored as text.

When the data is sorted quickly by the a-z or z-a button, things can go wrong. Whether the data contains a blank row or a blank column, some of the data will be sorted, and some will not. The best way to make sure you've picked the right data set before sorting is by giving it a name.

Excel expands the selection to a set (like pressing ctrl+shift+8) bounded by one or more blank columns and rows if a single cell is picked. The first row in the selected range is then examined to determine whether or not it contains the header information.

Column headers must comply with strict guidelines before they are accepted as headers by exc. For example, if the header row contains blank cells, excel may assume this isn't a header. Similarly, if the header row in the data set is formatted the same way as the other rows, then Excel can not recognize the header. Therefore, if a data table consists of text and the header row contains nothing but text, the header row would not be recognized by excel; the header row appears just like any data row.

Excel sorts only after the selection has been chosen, and excel decides whether the header row exists. The results of the sorting depend on whether excel has the right choice of range and the right determination of the header lines. For example, if excel does not think a header row exists, then the header is sorted into the data body.

To ensure that your data set is correctly recognized, use the shortcut ctrl+shift+8 to see what's selected to excel. If it does not meet your standards, either change the data character in your table or pick the data set before using the Sort dialogue.

To ensure that the headings are correctly understood, use the shortcut ctrl+shift+8 to pick the data set and then look at the first row. Unless the header has blank cells in the first row, the first row is formatted like the second row, or you have chosen more than one header row, then excel assumes that there is no header row. Make improvements to the header row to fix this and ensure that excel recognizes them.

If you use multi-row headers in your data table, excel may have trouble recognizing them. When you expect Excel to include blank rows in that header, the problem is compounded; it just can't do that automatically. However, you can pick the rows you want to sort before you do the sorting. In other words, be specific about what you want to sort out; don't let excel create the assumptions for you.

Days and times are stored as text.

If the date sorting results are not as expected, the data in the column containing the sort key may contain dates or times stored as text data rather than as numbers (dates and times are number formatted).

The record for a. In the picture above. Peterson ended up at the bottom of the list when, on the basis of the November 5, 2014 borrowing date, it would be above that for a. Wilson, who also has a November 5 borrowing date. The reason for the unexpected results is because the date of borrowing for a. Peterson was stored as a file, instead of as a number.

Mixed data and quick kinds

Excel sorts the number and text data separately by using a simple sorting method for records containing text and number data and places records for text data at the bottom of the sorted list.

Excel may also include the column headings in the results of the sorting, viewing them as just another row of text data instead of the field names for the data table.

Warnings sorted

Excel can show an alert when using the Sort dialogue box, even for sorts on a single column, that it has found data stored as text and gives the following options:

Filter something that looks numerically like a number.

Order numbers and numbers which are stored separately as text.

The first choice positions the text data in the appropriate location for the results of the form. The second choice places at the bottom of the sort result the records containing text data, just as it does with fast sorts.

CONCLUSION

A spreadsheet as a set of information distributed in columns and rows increases the likelihood of faster and more precise calculations. Numbers, text, and formulas can be put together and presented in a fancy and attractive way so that the meaning behind the numbers could be easily understood.

While the charting engine of Excel has a comparatively poor reputation among users, the majority of this is due to a lack of information about how to use the engine, rather than a lack of functionality. Sure, we want major improvements in graphics quality, better support for true 3D contour and XYZ scatter plots, and a general redesign of the user interface to make the advanced techniques demonstrated in this chapter much more discoverable for the average user.

However, after testing the charting engine and thoroughly understanding the strategies presented here, we realize that the limits of Excel's charting capabilities lie in our imagination and ingenuity, rather than with Excel.

Do not go yet; One last thing to do

If you enjoyed this book or found it useful, I'd be very grateful if you'd post a short review on it. Your support really does make a difference, and I read all the reviews personally so I can get your feedback and make this book even better.

Thanks again for your support!